A GHOST HUNTER'S GUIDE TO ESSEX

Jessie K Payne

Ian Henry Publications

© Jessie Kestell Payne, 1987

First published 1987
Reset edition 1995

ISBN 0 86025 463 1

The portrait on the front cover is of Anne Turner, who was executed at Tyburn on 15th November, 1615, for witchcraft

Printed by
Rapide Design & Print, Ltd.
Threxton Industrial Estate
Watton
Norfolk IP23 6NG
for
Ian Henry Publications, Ltd.
20 Park Drive, Romford, Essex RM1 4LH

The Devil in Essex

According to old legends the Devil had a predilection for Essex and played quite a few pranks on its inhabitants at different times. He has been shut in three churches and run away with a bell from the third.

In a lonely and little-known part of Essex, Dengie Hundred, stands Stansgate Priory Farm. It was on a summer day when I first came to it over the long road from Steeple that crosses marshes blue with sea lavender and smelling of the sea. On the south bank of the Blackwater stands the Priory Farm. All that remains of a Cluniac priory, a cell of the great house of Lewes, founded by Ralph, son of Brien, holder of Stansgate at the Domesday Survey, is a few stones built up into a wall on the site of the church that was connected with the story of the Devil of Stansgate. The priory church was long used as a barn, but shortly after the Royal Commission on Historical Monuments, 1914-18, reported on the church fabric the farmer pulled it down and nobody troubled to stop him. Later he became alarmed at his offence, gathered up some of the stones and built the wall that is now to be seen. These fragments, surrounded by farm buildings and young pigs, once heard the devotions of monks and beneath the farmyard still rest their bones.

The story of the Devil of Stansgate is that a man was ploughing near the church when he found things were not going well and he could not get on with the work. In desperation he angrily declared that the Devil could have his soul if he would do the ploughing. Exasperated, he spoke hastily, saying what he did not really mean, but he was taken at his word. To his horror the Devil appeared and took the plough. The frightened man ran for sanctuary into the priory church, but the Devil followed him into the sacred building, so he leapt out through a window and the Devil just missed him. Until the church was pulled down in 1923 there were marks still to be seen on the stones supposed to have been made by the Devil's claws.

The field the man was ploughing is still called the Devil's Field and was not ploughed again until 1946, presumably for fear of the Devil.

Another version is that the Devil was caught inside the building and shut in. His captors went for assistance, but when they returned the Devil had gone, leaving his footprints as he scrambled through the high window.

At Runwell St Mary, near Wickford, there was a more serious visitation. The story has been handed down from generation to generation and the late Rev Dr J E Bazille-Corbin assiduously collected and pieced together all the details. As with many old legends it is now falling into oblivion with the modern way of life and the building of new houses, whose occupants have no roots in the area and little interest in the old traditions.

On the inside of the 15th century south door of the parish church of Our Lady of the Running Well is the very clear impression, as of the palm of a left hand, burnt into the wood; this is said to be the Devil's claw mark (It certainly looks like the impressions of a claw-like hand).

In the middle of the 15th century, which is the approximate date of the door, the Rector of Runwell was ill and a priest, by name Rainaldus, chaplain of Lynsfords in Runwell[1], officiated for him. Rainaldus had an evil reputation and was said to practice Black Magic. Thus, with the Devil in his heart, it was that he was celebrating Mass one summer evening in the Jesus (or South) Chapel, when the Evil One suddenly issued from out of his mouth in visible form to the great terror both of the priest and his little congregation. The lay folk fled precipitately out by the north door, led by the parish clerk. The Devil chased Rainaldus from the altar and down the aisles ran Rainaldus pursued by the foul fiend, at last he reached the south door, standing open on this warm summer day. Although impeded by his vestments Rainaldus just managed to pass through the doorway and to draw the heavy door to behind him even as the outstretched left arm of the Evil One was about to clutch his shoulder. As he drew the door to and collapsed on the brick floor of the porch the palm of the Satanic hand smote on the woodwork and became imprinted thereon[2].

The Devil was now shut within the church. He could not pass over any of the three thresholds, as each had at the consecration of the building been aspersed with Holy Water. Defeated and imprisoned the Devil raged about the church wreaking fearful havoc. At last he escaped by hurling himself through the wall.

Meanwhile the parish clerk who had been serving the Mass had roused the Rector who left his sick bed and came running with the clerk to the church. In the south wall of the Jesus Chapel the newly made opening, some six inches square, was found. But what of Rainaldus? There was no recognisable trace of him! When they reached the South Porch all they found was a pool of eddying black evil-smelling liquid, which, as they watched in horror, began to sink into the floor of the porch, leaving in its wake a small flint about the size of a human hand, but bearing the well-defined shape of the hideous face of one long dead.

The opening made by Satan in his escape was sprinkled thrice with Holy Water in the form of a Cross and ordered by the Rector to be filled up with lime and a stone to be set either end. Thus it remained until 1944, when it was re-opened. It was perfectly obvious from outside, being framed in stone and so outlined and frequently pointed out to visitors. Archæologists, however, say it is a hagioscope through which the Elevation of the Host and Chalice might be viewed from the churchyard.

The hole being closed, the flint was set in the south wall of the Chapel in a large circle of black around which was painted in red letters "Stipendia peccati mores" (Romans VI,23) [For the wages of sin is death].

Another version of the story is that Rainaldus dropped dead and was buried under the stone at the entrance to the north porch, but Fr Corbin preferred the first ending as being more dramatic.

It is alleged that, after having been set in the wall for roughly a hundred years, Rainaldus's 'death mask' was thrown into the churchyard at the Reformation, being regarded at an item of superstition. In 1944, while edging one of the paths outside the Jesus Chapel, Fr Corbin and his youngest son, Christopher, unearthed a flint in the shape of an ugly twisted face, which he believed to be that of the legend and all that remained of Rainaldus. This strange flint was kept in a locked cupboard in the aisle of the church. Later it was restored to its original place in the wall, but in 1982 was taken out by order of the Church Council.

The oblong, almost coffin-shaped stone, broken in two halves and set as a doorstep of the North porch is always a 'cold spot', even in warm weather. When the Rector came to Runwell in 1923 the older generation of the parish would not venture to tread on this stone, but took care to step over it, and Fr Corbin thought that the fact that the stone in later years was trodden on accounts for the ghost of Rainaldus having been seen after a quiet period of about seventy years.

About a hundred years ago he is said to have appeared, but was not seen again until 1945, when an elderly couple saw him. Since then at least six different people said that they have seen him, the appearances generally being between January and April. The apparition is described as that of a tall man in either a black or brown habit, bare feet and with a cowl over his head, unshaven scarred face, deep set eyes and a very unpleasant expression.

A churchgoer in January, 1954, was out with her dog when she noticed a shadow and then felt as if someone unearthly passed through her body. Her dog was terrified, ran home and whimpered for most of the night. Mr B L Lester Crook told me his experience: it was after Evensong on a Sunday in March, 1954, at about 8.30, when it was quite dark. As he passed the lighted telephone box by the churchyard he thought he saw a shadow against the fence of 'Ilgars'. The shadow seemed rather odd in appearance, standing out from the fence. He stopped and moved several yards side to side, but the shadow did not move. Mr Crook then felt a chilly 'tingling' sensation in his spine and his stomach turned over. The shadow then apparently of its own accord moved off down the fence and vanished by the barn. Although the light from the telephone kiosk does throw one's shadow eerily against the fence, Mr Crook distinctly saw a figure which, although it resembled a shadow at first sight, was, on closer examination, a vague form hovering about a foot from the ground and a yard away from the fence.

Rainaldus was seen in daylight by Mr H P Liberty, Lord of the Manor of Runwell, who was driving his car towards Wickford about 10 o'clock in the morning, when he was amazed to see 'a clerical figure dressed in a grey overcoat, black homburg hat, knee breeches and stockings and wearing a dog collar - obviously an ordinary reverend gentleman - but following him a few paces behind was a broad shouldered, slouching figure, dressed in a dark brown habit reaching almost to the ground, secured with what appeared to be a broad leather belt, and wearing a tight-fitting cap from which emerged somewhat unkempt hair, growing down the sides of the face to a thin beard, but extending well across the cheek bones. I immediately stopped the car, jumped out and looked up the road (having passed them by this time) the road was completely empty! In the course of a day or so I told Father Corbin, who was interested and con firmed that at noon the same day a clerical friend, wearing the clothes described, had in fact visited him.'

Mr Liberty saw the ghost twice more. On the second occasion he saw Rainaldus in the churchyard quite clearly and for some seconds near the West Door. In 1955 he again saw Rainaldus apparently following the Rector along the footpath bordering the churchyard and this at a time when, on enquiry, he found that the Rector was certainly not there! Mr Liberty was driving his car in the direction of Wickford as the visions appeared, he drew up quickly and remained stationary until the figures passed and disappeared. He described the Rector as wearing a black cape lined with red silk over his cassock. He noted this particularly, as he had never seen Father Corbin wearing it, although he often did so in cold weather.

In 1954 a man from Great Burstead told Father Corbin that in the daytime he had seen a figure in a brown robe, with a scar on his face and with terribly piercing eyes, walking down the road between the church and Wickford. He was followed a very short way behind by a priest wearing a black silk cassock.

One explanation as to why Rainaldus and other ghostly visitors in the church and its neighbourhood had become more frequent at that time was that at the 11 o'clock Sunday service the old Sarum Mass (in English) was being used. This was the rite of the Middle Ages and seems to have stirred up the psychic forces in (maybe) a pleasurable manner, as they found a familiar rite in almost all respects as they once knew it and in the same surroundings. To restore a building to its former aspect apparently does sometimes attract its former occupants: the interior of Runwell church was largely as it had been five centuries ago, with coloured screen as in mediæval times, a statue of Our Lady standing in the niche behind the High Altar and the Jesus Chapel refurnished, St Peter's Altar replaced and the building restored to its original state in many ways.

A quaint Devil legend about Runwell is given in *Notes and Queries* for 11 July, 1857. The builder of the church is said to have fought three pitched battles with the foul fiend and beat him each time. "The devil, finding he could not vanquish the man living, said he would have him at all events, when dead, whether buried in the church he was building or out of it. To elude this, he ordered himself to be buried half in the church and half out of it." There is a tomb in the north wall of the chancel, but it is said to be of an early 14th century Prioress of the supposed 'Convent of the Running Well', situated at Poplars Farm, Runwell.

On the Stock Road, Billericay, was formerly a ramshackle cottage that took some time to build as every morning the materials erected the day before were scattered on the ground, apparently by ghostly means. Perhaps this too was the Devil's work.

In 1402 on the feast of Corpus Christi the Devil in the shape and habit of a Minorite Friar is said to have entered Danbury Church. The nave and aisles and part of the chancel were destroyed in the ensuing thunderstorm, but the damage was attributed to the evil one who 'raged insolently' in the church.

The Devil came back to Danbury, if the *Gentleman's Magazine* of 1896 can be believed, for it is stated that he had a special animosity against the fifth bell (now the sixth) of the peal. For a long time no Danbury man would ring it. It appears that this took the place of a bell stolen from the tower by the Devil. For some reason or other he had to drop the bell - one version being that he carried it in a kink in his tail, but while taking it to his home in Maldon, the knot loosened and the bell fell in Bell Hill Wood and there it is believed to be hidden. A pond here is said to have been caused by the fall of the bell and folks used to visit it in the hope of seeing the Devil. Mrs Hopkirk in her *History of Danbury* says that she thinks this happened between 1618 and 1622, but that it is possible that it was stolen by scrap iron merchants, who hid it in the woods when they were discovered.

The Devil legend of Tolleshunt Knights and Virley is well known and assumed various forms.

Briefly, the story that belongs equally to the two villages is that when in the Devil's Wood in Virley they dug a moat and started to build a house, a man with his three spey bitches was left on guard all night. The first night the Devil came and said, "Who is there?" and the man answered, "God and myself and my three spey bitches", and the Devil departed. The second night the same thing happened, but the third night the man forgot himself and answered, "Myself, my three spey bitches and God", thus putting himself the wrong way round. So the Devil clawed the heart out of the man's body, then he took a beam from the house and said, as he threw it up the hill,

>Where this beam shall fall
>There shall ye build Barnhall.

The Devil vowed he would have the man's soul whether he was buried in the church or out of it, but was cheated by burying the man half in and half out of the wall of Tolleshunt Knights church. Some say the Devil came by night and destroyed the work of the day, so a knight attended by two dogs kept watch; when the Devil appeared a tussle ensued when the Devil hurled the beam.

Yet another version is that Barn Hall was to be built in the wood, but every morning the lord of the manor found the previous day's work undone, so he decided to watch. At midnight the Evil One appeared, accompanied by two dogs, and enquired what he did there. When told he watched to see who destroyed the building, the Devil took up a beam, throwing it to the top of the hill a mile away, where Barn Hall now stands.

The story is sometimes preceded by a statement that it

was because the wood was used for the Devil's revels that he was angry at the building. This may refer to Devil worship, as in early days small numbers of people did practise unsavoury rites in lonely places and this may have been one of them. Ragstone rubble foundations in the Devil's Wood point to a house once standing on the site, possibly the de Patteshalls rebuilt on higher ground because it was healthier. Ague was prevalent on the marshy lands of Essex, so perhaps the legend is a fusion of two stories, the rebuilding on higher ground and memories of Black Magic on the abandoned site in Devil's Wood.

In Barn Hall, which was reconstructed in 1800, is still the Devil's Beam with the reputed marks of Satan's claws, really mortice peg holes. It is a moulded 15th century beam. No one can damage it, it is said, without hurting himself. Within living memory it has been touched 'for a cure'.

In All Saints, Tolleshunt Knights, is a tomb half in the wall, now said to be that of the knight Atte Lee, who died in 1385, but for long it was associated with de Patteshalls of Barnhall. Scratches on the tomb have been pointed out as made by the Devil trying to get at the knight's body. The Devil's two dogs are also said to be seen roaming the marshes at night. When Tolleshunt Knights church became redundant it was given to the Greek Monastery of St John the Baptist.

In Wix churchyard is a cage containing an ancient bell, once belonging to the nunnery that flourished until it was suppressed and its income given towards building and endowing Cardinal Wolsey's college at Oxford. The story goes that the tower of the nuns' church was built three times and as many times the Devil pulled it down at night.

Finally they put the bell in a cage and the Devil agreed to leave it alone.

The north sides of churchyards were often associated with the Devil and the oldest tombstones in most churchyards will therefore be found to the south of the church. Unbaptised children and suicides were put on the north. The origin of the belief that the south side was better antedates Christianity when the sun was venerated as the source of light and heat and it was thought that all evil spirits would flee before it, so the north, the sunless, cold side, was shunned. The old Norse hell lay in the north.

In a number of Essex churches there is a blocked-in door on the north wall opposite the font; this is some times called the Devil's Door, through which the Devil is said to have escaped when driven out of infants being baptised. There are such doors at Basildon, Great Wakering, and Vange, among others.

Mrs F B Clark wrote to tell me that Goldacres Farm, a 16th century house in Thorrington, is supposed to be haunted by 'Old Nick', who comes even in daylight. Some people living have claimed to have seen him looking like a tramp wearing a cloak. The present owner of the farm is simply amused and, when the doors rattle in the wind, he says, "It's Old Nick," and calls, "Come in." When Mrs Clark tried to find out more about the apparition, one elderly lady, evidently a firm believer in such things, started to quarrel with her over the matter. "These things are true and should not be pried into," the old lady said.

At Steeple there is the Devil's Marsh and on Wallasea Island was formerly the Devil's House, where once some men were thrown out of bed and a man is said to have seen the Devil on Wallasea Marshes, though a more populous area would be a better hunting ground for Satan. The Devil's House was also said to be haunted by the ghost of a witch's familiar, which was rather like an ape. The sound of wings would be heard and a room would become intensely cold.

Jarvis Hall, Thundersley, is also said to have had a visit from his Satanic Majesty: the story goes that one wintry night the Devil, seeking shelter from the gales he had made, knocked at the door of Jarvis Hall, still standing not far from Bread and Cheese Hill. But inside were priests, hiding from soldiers as their religion had been banned (obviously dating in the reigns of Henry VIII or Mary) and as soon as they opened the door, the Devil took fright and ran down a slope called from that day the Devil's Steps. It was said to be impossible for anyone ever to go to sleep in old Jarvis Hall barn - not because of the Devil, but because it was said to be faithfully visited by the spirits of the ancient departed ones of the place, their presence making it out of the question for anyone to close their eyes in the building.

[1] **Lynsfords in Runwell was pulled down in 1870 by Thomas Kemble of Runwell Hall. It was where the steward of the Manor of Runwell lived. In the 15th century the lords of the manor were the Dean and Chapter of St Paul's. The chapel at Lynsfords is an historical fact and Rainaldus was Chaplain there at the time of the story.**

[2] **Fr Corbin told me that the Devil is always supposed to use his left hand in preference to his right in dealing with mortals.**

Queer happenings in ancient churches

Even in these enlightened days there are many who would not like to spend a night in an ancient church. In some Essex churches there would be good reason for not doing so, as strange things happen in them.

At Borley church, opposite the site of the famous Borley Rectory that was said to be the most haunted house in England, there have been a number of unexplained occurrences. Music and a choir have often been heard in the building at night when it was known to be both empty and locked. A man heard singing or chanting coming from the church when it was in complete darkness. When the Rev Hemming was rector he was passing the church one day when he heard the organ playing, but investigation revealed no one there.

On 9th August, 1949, the Rev C S Kipling, who had known Borley all his life and disbelieved stories of its haunting, went to the church to read the lesson at the funeral of a friend. It was a lovely sunny day and, after making preparations, he went to the door to see if any one was arriving; then he saw the figure of a girl, slight in build and about twenty years old, very heavily veiled. As he looked at her she vanished. He had no doubt that he had seen the ghostly nun who haunted the precincts of Borley Rectory [*Essex Chronicle,* 2 September, 1949].

Mr G Ashard of Alpheton, Sudbury, wrote to the *Essex Weekly News* on 30 September, 1949, stating his son's experiences at Borley Church.

"Most of the working class people do not believe in the haunting at Borley, so I asked my two sons and a friend to go over and see if there was anything. They went on Saturday night, September 10. It was a grand night - full moon and very quiet. They arrived there about 9 p.m. and sat in the church porch looking for the Veiled Girl. At 9.45 something dropped in the church. Then about 10 p.m. they heard a creaking noise as if a door was being slowly opened in the church. The door slammed and then there was an unearthly rumbling noise lasting about five minutes. They tried the door, but it was locked. Then they looked through the windows with a bright torch and there was no one there. It was a warm night, but it seemed cold in the Church porch. We now know for sure that all that has been said is true. We intend to pay further visits and feel sure we shall see the Veiled Girl and many other things. My sons' ages are 21 and 17 and the friend's age is 17."

A former Rector's daughter, Miss Ethel Bull, told the late Harry Price that many years ago some coffins in the church crypt had been displaced, "They were all higgledy piggledy and no normal explanation was forthcoming..."

Some plate was removed from Borley church at the time of the Reformation and it is supposed to be buried on the Rectory site.

The ghost of the infamous Bishop Bonner, the last Roman Catholic Bishop of London, is supposed to appear at different times in Copford church, descending from the altar steps in ecclesiastical robes and carrying his staff. He is said to be buried under the High Altar. Nearby Copford Hall was a private residence of the Bishops of London.

Bonner, fearing that valuable church plate might be confiscated by the reformers, is supposed to have hidden some in a secret tunnel between the hall and the church. A woman cleaner at the church told Mr A Morrish of Chelmsford that she often heard mysterious noises during the daytime of footsteps walking the aisle and up to the pulpit, the banging of the pulpit and of a book and the slamming of a church door.

An organ tuner was discussing Bishop Bonner with a local lad who was assisting him in the church. The lad laughed at what he considered to be just a yarn, where upon some old dusty books that had not been used for many years, slid off his seat, moved as by unseen hands.

The *Essex Weekly* published a story in May, 1950, that five local residents of Cressing testified to their belief that during the winter months some ghostly visitant had persisted in playing weird symphonies on the organ in the dark behind the locked doors of their 13th century church. With the consent of the Vicar two members of the Braintree Fire Service made plans to watch for the spectre. For two nights they sat in the church from dusk to dawn, but not a thing did they see or hear. Two more nights with the moon nearly full they sat in a secluded hideout in the church without result. Nevertheless, the villagers were unshaken in their belief that late night and early morning voluntaries were played on the organ by a phantom organist, as the building was locked and no unauthorised person could gain access.

At the lonely little church of St Margaret's, Bowers Gifford, it is also said that the organ is heard at night when the building is empty. Some years ago the son of a friend of mine heard the rumour and he and three other boys visited the church one summer evening. They took it in turns to sit in the church alone. As he sat in the dim, silent church, the only living person in the building, the organ suddenly began to play. He fled outside to his companions and was very upset for days afterwards.

Mrs M Bettany of South Benfleet and a friend visited Bowers Gifford church one day. As they entered Mrs Bettany saw standing two pews down on the south side of the church an old man with a short white beard, who looked like a clergyman. She was laughing at something that had amused her and the old man glared at her and looked as if he was extremely angry that she should behave thus in the holy edifice. Mrs Bettany says that she felt rather foolish, lowered her voice and walked with her friend towards the vestry. The church door was shut, but when they turned round the man had gone. Still feeling rather annoyed Mrs Bettany said, "Let's go out" and when they reached the churchyard she remarked that the man in the church had been most annoyed with her for laughing. "What man?" asked her friend, "There was no man in the church."

Members of the Phenomenist Research League from Southend on Sea visited Bowers Gifford church one autumn night in 1956 to obtain evidence about the phantom organist. They reported that they saw and felt presences and that there were some very chilly psychic draughts, one 'presence' in the form of a vicar in his surplice was very strong and kept appearing.

It is also said that the church has a crypt that has not been opened for over two hundred years; even the wardens do not know the situation at which the entrance is to be found.

Besides the story of Rainaldus related in the previous chapter, Runwell church has three other stories connected with it.

Christopher Peacock was the parish clerk at Runwell in the time of Charles I and used to climb the turret stairs daily to see whether Roundhead troops were approaching in order to warn his master, the rector, Simon Lynch, a staunch Royalist. His footsteps are some times heard mounting the stairs and the late Rector, Rev Dr. J E Bazille-Corbin himself heard them.

Other stories given to me by the Rector are -

From time to time cracking, creaking and banging noises as tho' some timber structure was being moved, hit or split appear to come from the pews and chancel screen. Whatever the more prosaic explanation, it is nevertheless said that these are the echoes of the sounds made at the time when the 'carved work' of the original screen which spanned the chancel was hacked to pieces and destroyed 'with axes and hammer' by the Roundhead soldiery. The second sound that from time to time makes itself apparent is as though someone was sitting down, rising up, and moving from pew to pew, unable to settle comfortably in any one spot. This seemingly restless worshipper is said to be Anne, Lady Sulyard (the only member of the family whom the Registers record as being buried here, and not in the graveyard at Flemings or in the manorial chapel). In her day it is understood that a family pew was installed for the first time and it took her a considerable time to decide which position she would have it fixed. She died almost immediately after the pew was set up, but apparently had never been satisfied that it occupied the best of positions, and so restlessly moves from place to place, trying out first by sitting, then by kneeling or standing at each possible spot. Anne, daughter of William Eden of Sudbury, married Sir Edward Sulyard of Flemings - died 1620. There is no memorial to her in the church.

On the day I met the Rector in 1955 he told me that he had heard Lady Sulyard and the creaking pew that morning. While we were talking in the church there was a creak and the Rector said, "That was Lady Sulyard".

Only a fragment of the large mansion of Flemings, Lady Anne's old home, remains. It dates from about 1600 and originally contained a chapel, but the major portion of the house is said to have been destroyed by fire; it is now a farmhouse. Two rooms were discovered over one of the bedrooms with a quantity of straw, but lacking floorboards.

A vision of the Holy Virgin is said to have been seen at Middleton church in 1932 and 1933; All Saints was originally dedicated to St Mary the Virgin. Early communicants saw a vision of a beautiful woman on a Sunday in February, 1933. She is said to have been seen many times and was known as Our Lady by those who had seen her. At dusk on a December day in 1932 the vision was seen by the Rector and others from the Rectory dining-room standing on a little mound just outside the low wall of the lawn. Stars and light appeared to be round her head. One man, a churchwarden, is said to have approached quite close to the figure and fell on his knees with head bowed, the figure raising her hands as if in blessing. Someone connected with psychic research is also said to have seen frescos of the Holy Virgin appear on the church wall.

In 1921 a hard-headed businessman saw an objective vision of Christ crucified in Braintree parish church. The *Daily Express* on 8 October, 1921, reported that the Rev W J L Sheppard, Vicar of Holy Trinity, Ripon, who had been conducting mission services in the church, stated from the pulpit that 'during the evening service last Sunday a well-known Braintree business man who was seated in the congregation, saw a vision of the crucified Saviour in the chancel of the church. Next morning the man confided in me and the Vicar of Braintree what he had seen. He said that he first saw the vision while he was kneeling in prayer. The bright light from the halo on the head of the crucified Christ filled the whole church and blotted out every other object. This was not the case of an emotional woman seeing a vision, but a practical man. The vision must be taken as a divine revelation to the Mission'.

Both the Rev D B Barclay, Vicar of Braintree, and the Rev Sheppard were quite satisfied that the man did see the vision. He said that when he first saw the vision he bowed his head to collect his thoughts and make quite sure of himself. Then he looked up again and the vision of Christ crucified still filled the chancel. He looked at it for about four minutes the second time, then the light from the halo gradually faded and the vision disappeared. The figure was quite distinct on the Cross. The vision did not speak or beckon, but looked at him with pleading eyes. The man became quite ill and broke into a violent perspiration.

The ancient church of Ashingdon is built on the site of a battlefield, for here on Ashingdon Hill the Danish King, Canute, fought Edmond Ironside and was victorious in 1016. Four years later Canute, according to the *Anglo Saxon Chronicle*, "caused to be built there a minster of stone and lime for the souls of the men who there were slain". Stigand, Archbishop of Canterbury from 1052-70, was the first priest. Ashingdon church stands on the site of this minster and possibly contains some stones from it. In June, 1951, it was restored and rededicated, when Prince Georg of Denmark attended the rededication service, probably the first Royal visitor since Canute came to the consecration of the minster.

Such an ancient and historic church it would seem must have some ghostly phenomena. A gentleman, very level-headed and entirely trustworthy, but who did not wish his name to appear, told me that during much of the time he was connected with Ashingdon church he had frequent subjective visions in the church: and this is what he said:

I saw literally scores of individuals, many of them dressed in costumes centuries old. Some appeared in the nave, but most in the chancel, all during divine service. The most prolific period was during the two or three weeks following the re-dedication, when a whole lot of men in Danish armour appeared, also a beautiful woman who seemed to be clad in a wonderful blue light. Once, while I was actually kneeling at the Communion rail, I saw an Eastern man on the right side of the altar; he was clad in a wonderful dark purple robe. I was worried at the time about my sister, who was in hospital with internal trouble. I sought his help. My sister survived a major operation and was completely restored to health.

One Sunday, during the 11 o'clock service, I saw a sturdy looking monk in the prime of manhood issue from the tower and stand gazing towards the East end. He was dressed in brown habit and sandals.

I attended the funeral of Mr ..., who was organist at Ashingdon for many years. During the service inside the church he appeared in the nave, dressed in his surplice as usual and holding a book. He was facing the congregation and looking rather puzzled. A little later, during the committal in the churchyard, I saw him standing by the graveside.

Thundersley church was associated with a restless spirit for two generations. Near a 400 years old elm tree in the churchyard is the grave of a murdered man, who, by disturbing the early morning with his cry, gave the Rectory the reputation of being a haunted spot.

The Rev. E A B Maley, late Rector of Thundersley, in *The Ancient Parish of Thundersley,* tells how, one winter morning while it was still dark, the occupant of a thatched cottage near the church heard two men go by quarrelling. They went through the churchyard and she heard some scuffling when they reached a gate standing near the elm and later she heard a great cry. The church register states that Harry Witney, a stranger found dead on the road, was buried in January, 1871. His murderer died in an asylum after telling the story that had unhinged his mind. Thereafter came the cry at ten minutes to seven every morning - "a mingling of the moan of one in physical pain and the shriek of a lost soul. Witney, the Rev Maley suggests, by provoking his murderer may have encompassed his own death.

Someone from the Psychical Research Society suggested that the sounds came from the white owls that lived in a nearby walnut tree. Later the owls left for the woods, but the early morning cry did not cease. When it did, there was an explanation.

Mr Maley noticed that the cry did not come on Sunday mornings nor on Thursdays after there began the custom of a special celebration of Holy Communion. on the one hand for those who had lost their friends and also for friends lost and the sick. After a time the cries ceased for good.

Romford has a legend of ghostly church bells. The old church of St Andrews was pulled down some five centuries ago. Hornchurch had been the only church in the Liberty of Havering, then the Prior of Hornchurch applied to Edward II for permission to build a chapel of ease at Romford. Leave being granted, the chapel of St Andrew was built near the River Rom, which overflowed its banks and sapped the foundations. The town grew and the chapel became too small, so in 1406 Henry IV granted by Charter the site in Market Place and the old chapel was deserted. It stood in Old Church Road and the legend is that the ancient chapel sank into the ground and that, every year on St Andrew's Day at noon, the bells may be heard pealing merrily.

The old church at Walton-on-the-Naze was swept away by the encroachments of the sea in 1798, but its ghostly bells are said to be heard tolling under the sea at certain times, foretelling bad weather. In January, 1928, the church suddenly reappeared in consequence of an extraordinary low tide following a storm. It was thickly covered with shells and seaweed; some thought it was a submarine upheaval, but it was the 'ghost' church. Crowds flocked to see it and some tried to cross the sands to the church, but were prevented by doing so by the soft sands and the incoming tide. The church was visible for a few hours only, then it was engulfed by the sea once more.

There is a strange legend connected with the grave just

outside the main church door in Brightlingsea churchyard of a former atheist, John Selletto of Harwich, who was buried in 1771. On his deathbed Selletto was surrounded by friends who implored him to believe in God, but he refused absolutely to do so and made a strange prophecy. "When I am buried," he said, "If there is a God, an ash tree will grow up from my grave."

No one thought much of the prophecy until years later, when the tombstone over his grave started to crack and then a young ash tree came through the side of the tomb and flourished, fulfilling the atheist's saying. It tilted the stone to a dangerous angle, until about 1941, when the tomb became so dangerous that the tree had to be removed. When digging out the roots, the skull and bones of the atheist were disinterred and some bright schoolboys took the skull to their science master, but the Vicar was soon on their track and it was duly restored to the churchyard.

A similar story is told of a tomb in Clavering churchyard, only this time it was a lady who died in the 17th century who said that if there was a Heaven and Hall an ash and maple would grow above her grave and, according to whether an ash or a maple grew out of the tomb, so would her soul be in Heaven or Hell. An ash tree has grown and split the tombstone.

Benton in the *History of Rochford Hundred* tells of an altar tomb in Prittlewell churchyard sacred to the memory of Samuel Brown, Esq., who died 15th November, 1827, aged 30 years, and other members of the Brown family. Some time after Samuel's burial crowds of people came to the churchyard and watched the tomb, believing that they could hear a noise within.

In Rayne churchyard there is, or was, a plain upright

tombstone near the tower. The inscription defaced by time formerly read

Sacred to the Memory of
John Joslin June 5th, 1800, Aged 48 years.

This I have done for a
Kind and indulgent husband
Near and Dear to me.
And it is nothing to you
What I have done
Or what I do

The story goes that at the end of the 18th century and in the beginning of the 19th, there was a lady in Rayne, who married three husbands and all three were said to have died because the wife put pigeons' feathers in their pillows which, according to the old superstition, drew the life away. The second husband did not live long and, before he died, he threatened that his spirit would 'walk' if she married again.

However, it was not long before the widow did want to marry again, but she was scared that if she did her husband's ghost would haunt her, so she decided on an ancient form of incantation. At dusk she took some friends to the churchyard and, while they waited at the gate, she went to the grave. Here she stood at the head facing east and, pointing to herself she said, "I" and then pointing to the spot: "John Joslin! May I marry again?" Then she walked round the grave 'the way of the sun'. Three times she did this and then waited for an answer.

She neither heard nor saw anything, but was not dismayed for she interpreted it as 'silence gives consent' and she married again, but, before she did so, she erected the gravestone with its strange inscription, both propitiatory and defiant [*Essex Review,* January, 1938].

At Hockley the local people say that long, long ago a beautiful lady was riding through the village in a coach when the horses swerved and the coach crashed into a tree, the lady and the driver being killed outright. The rumour is that at certain times of the year the coach with its four white horses returns and passes the nearby church. The lady orders the driver to pull up and then she waves her white gloved hands at any passer-by. The coach then travels on and repeats the tragedy. The Phenomenist Research League from Southend-on-Sea visited Hockley in August, 1956, to find out if there was any truth in the rumours of the phantom coach. All the members of the expedition agreed that it was the most eerie place they had visited. They all had 'strange inexplicable experiences'. Several heard very peculiar sounds and two reported seeing a 'shape' moving on the church tower. A large white figure dashed past them. "It could have been a rabbit," said Mr Godfrey-Bartram, "but it was very large too large for a rabbit in my opinion." Everyone agreed that the atmosphere 'was unearthly' said Garry Spencer, the secretary of the League.

The Phenomenist League also organised a 'ghost hunt' at St Nicholas Church, Canewdon, in August, 1957. The churchwarden, who had been in the choir for well over 60 years, told members of the expedition that it is said that if a person circles the church alone at midnight the witches and ghosts will come out and sing to them. Although each member in turn walked round the church they spotted no spectres; it was not midnight, but there was an 'atmosphere' on the oldest side of the church, the west side. Several members of the party experienced a strange psychic 'cold' near the altar, as if a barrier had been drawn across the north end of the church and the atmosphere was distinctly different to that elsewhere in the church. Two members saw a weird aura of light surrounding the top of the tower lasting only a few seconds.

Mr P B Godfrey-Bartram carried out a colour test and a vibration test. The former is a small bottle of blue liquid containing strontium and various other ingredients and will usually turn black if there is psychic influence in ti!e area. The vibration test is a bottle of mercury and will vibrate if there is a strong 'influence' prevailing. Both tests showed negative. This was expected, as it was too early for anything to happen.

One of the ghosts of Canewdon churchyard is said to be that of a headless woman dressed in silk, some say they have seen her riding on a hurdle down the hill from the church to the river, where she disappears, but appears again on the other side of the water.

Another version is that the ghost of a woman dressed in a crinoline and poke bonnet rises from a tomb in the churchyard and goes down the lanes to the river bank. She had not been seen for many years, when she suddenly reappeared on the far side of the river, minus bonnet and head and floating before the hearth of an old house!

In 1964 local people claimed to have seen the ghost of a hooded red monk move across Church Road, Basildon, and vanish into the churchyard. One person who claimed to see the apparition said, "the second time I saw the monk I cycled right through him. The air was cold and clammy. I went numb all over and could not speak".

It is interesting that two of the former priests of Holy Cross, Basildon, who were later consecrated bishops, had also been monks. James Daren [1483] was a Franciscan and John Hodgeskynne [1544] was a Dominican.

Rev B Lloyd, curate at Basildon at the time, said he never saw the ghost, although often at the church, but sometimes in the daylight and at night when in the church, he had thought somebody had walked into the porch, hesitate to come in and was waiting outside, but on opening the door he found no one there, but he felt this could be readily explained, as birds scuffling in the roof or "some such thing".

St Nicholas, Canewdon, at the turn of the century

Uncanny happenings in Essex homes

A terrible experience in an old house in the Brightlingsea neighbourhood was told by an aunt of mine. On Boxing morning, 1945, she woke as it was getting light and became aware that the bedclothes were slowly rising up beside her, then an icy cold form pressed itself close to her side. She was terror stricken and quite unable to move, hut she did manage to gasp out, "Oh, go away, go away!" The form stayed for some minutes then slowly, very slowly, the thing went. Feeling shocked, but extremely relieved, my aunt got out of bed and looked everywhere, including under the bed, but nothing was to be seen. On complaining to her hosts they discredited her story and said that nothing like it had happened before, but she was too frightened to stay and left to spend the following night at a friend's house at Thorrington.

On a quiet country road in the Maldon area is a 16th century house possessing a lively ghost. The house has an unhappy history and had frequently changed hands; servants leave because they see or hear the ghost. At some unknown date two sisters lived there. The younger sister stole the elder's young man and married him. Later she came to stay at the house and the elder sister had her revenge by smothering her in bed. The ghost has been seen standing at a window when the house was empty and a clergyman felt it pushing him down the drive when he wanted to go up it! It was like a blast of air he said. He prayed and persisted, it was just like a nightmare, and at last he gained the house, when the terrible feeling ceased.

Two foreign maids speaking no English, who could not have known the story, were frightened and left because they used to hear the ghost stump upstairs to their room and then felt her pull the bedclothes off. Children who were put to bed in the house asked why their parents kept coming up the stairs and walking down the corridor, when, in fact, nobody had done so. A footman fell or jumped out of the haunted room window having been chased by the ghost and died as a result of the fall.

About 1917 a lady went to the house to leave an invitation to a tennis party. She experienced a very creepy feeling as she walked up the drive and no one answered the door when she knocked. Something made her look up at the house and she saw at a window a most horrible face, with long grey hair. Numb with terror, she threw the note in the porch and fled, but the thing at the window did not move. Later, when she met the lady of the house, she mentioned that she could not make anyone hear, although the housekeeper was in, but she was told no one was in and the house had been empty.

A house dating back to Cromwellian days in Southend has, or perhaps it should be said had, a spectre of a beautiful bride, not seen for many years now. The ghost was said to be of a lovely auburn-haired girl attired in a white bridal gown. In 1934 one of the occupants of the house asserted that he did not believe in the story when he was told about the ghost by the previous tenants. One winter evening about 9 o'clock he was approaching the house when he saw the figure of a young girl with flowing reddish hair wearing what appeared to be a full length white bridal gown standing under a big tree in front of the house. The figure was luminous in the dark and, as he watched, it appeared to drift into a nearby meadow. This severely shocked him and he finally reached the house by a roundabout route.

A lady said that her mother, who was a most practical woman, used to live in the house and three times saw the ghost. The spare room many years ago was known as the 'ghost room' and a blind girl slept there once and, on being asked the next morning how she had slept, had replied that, "Someone in the room kept putting a hand over my face". The room was not used as a bedroom after that. Many people have said that they have seen or heard the ghost. The apparition never hurt anyone and more or less kept to one oak-beamed room in the oldest part of the house. She had a habit of fastening doors and locking people in their rooms. One gentleman found himself imprisoned in his bedroom when he got up one morning. Another found himself locked in a room when he was the only person in the house! It is hard to believe that in all cases the lock or bolt could have fallen into position on its own.

When the family were all in one room they had heard noises as if someone was walking down the passage and doors were heard to open and shut for no apparent reason. Investigations never revealed anything. A visitor, who was a stranger to the house, heard the front door open and shut, the hallstand rattle and footsteps come down the hallway. He went to the door, saying that it was his host returned home early. The sounds were heard by all in the room, but the house was empty and the host did not arrive until his usual time. The lady of the house several times had felt the spectre touch her. Why the mysterious bride, if bride she be, should haunt the house is unknown as there is no story to account for it. A former owner was, however, very eccentric.

Berechurch Hall, near Colchester, that was demolished in 1953, had a ghost, the 'Lady in White'. Berechurch Hall had a long and interesting history. Eudo Dapifer, the King's steward, gave it to the Abbey of St John in Colchester and. at the Dissolution of the Monasteries, it passed to the Lord Chancellor of England, Sir Thomas Audley. Eventually the manor passed into the hands of the Smythe family. In 1882 a Member of Parliament, Octavius Edward Coope, spent £50,000 in restoring the house. So much for the history of the Hall. This is the tale of the 'White Lady', as written by Mrs Chilvers, who, with her husband, was caretaker there.

Berechurch Hall was a beautiful mansion of 52 main rooms. It had originally been an old monastery and supposed to have a subterranean passage leading to St John's Abbey Gate. Its interior was lovely in times gone by. At the time of my living there it was practically empty of furniture. The huge dining room had a frieze right round it of life-sized cherubim holding garlands of flowers, and the big silver safe was built into one of the towers in the corner of the room. The marble mantlepiece was sculptured with eight episodes in the life of Hercules. The ballroom had a Venetian marble mantlepiece and an Adam ceiling. There was supposed to be a bullet hole under the paper over the ballroom fireplace, the result of a duel that was fought outside the ballroom window on the terrace. Whether the bloodstain often seen on the ballroom floor had anything to do with this duel I cannot say.

In the library was a most wonderful panel in tapestry showing a lady in flowing robes sitting by a swimming pool with her two Great Danes lying by her side, also her two serving maids playing lyres by her feet. That panel I understand has gone to America, but I always understood that whoever removed this panel a curse would descend on the said person, but I cannot vouch for the accuracy of this statement.

Now for the story of Charlotte, the 'Lady in White'. My husband and I had been caretaking for about four years when one evening some gentlemen turned up and said they had come to watch for the ghost. We had never seen or heard anything at that time and they were asked to depart. At that time we thought nothing of ghosts and yet folks used to ask us however we could live in such a huge, creepy place. Anyway, time passed by and one afternoon the front door bell rang. On answering it I found a lady on the step with her French maid or companion. I asked her in, as I did all visitors, so many came to view the old place. In course of conversation this lady, connected with the family who were the previous owners of the Hall, asked me if I had seen Charlotte. I replied, "No, madam, who is she?" I was then informed that Charlotte had lived in the Hall many years ago, and her husband dearly loved her, but she did him a wrong. He forgave her and, for a forgiveness present, gave her a lovely white satin gown edged with swansdown. The story this lady told me was that she had such regrets for the way in which she had treated her husband that she couldn't rest at nights and the lady said, "You know, they say she walked the Hall in life and she still walks it in death.

Have you seen her yet?" I very quickly answered, "No, I haven't." She then told me that somewhere across the park was Charlotte's swimming pool. We found it under a huge horse chestnut with two marble steps leading down to where the water used to be and a marble seat with a marble slab acting as a backrest, with the word 'CHORLETTE' carved in it. Scores of pretty seashells were let in round this place. I was told that Charlotte used to go swimming there and take with her the two Great Danes. She was supposed to have died in the rooms, or those built previous to the alterations, that we occupied as caretakers.

I was taken unawares the night I saw Charlotte. Some of the owners' family where in residence and I had cooked a late dinner, etc., and went out of the back door to call in my dear old black cat, Sambo. It was on a Thursday night and very often the groom's wife, who lived in the stables, would run out of sugar and would come to borrow some. This particular evening I called my cat and stood waiting for him to come in. It was fairly moonlit and I saw what I took to be the groom's wife coming down towards me. I watched her coming the whole length of the back drive and thought to myself what a long pinafore Mrs Taylor had on and what I took to be a shawl over her head. She glided along towards me and got to within a yard or two of me and then just lifted and, as she lifted from the earth, her robe just flared out a bit and gradually disappeared. I never saw a face. I then realised I had seen the 'Lady in White'! I felt as though I were numb, I walked the long corridor from the back door to our sitting room; just sat myself down. My husband asked me several times what was the matter. I just couldn't speak. I said nothing to anyone 'til about three weeks afterwards when my husband said to me "If the estate manager wants his stove lit up in his bedroom, promise me you won't go upstairs after it gets dusk." I said, "Why?", but my husband refused to say any further till I said, "Oh, have you seen her too?" Then he told me he had gone up to light this oilstove and had seen Charlotte come down from our bedroom over the ballroom along the corridor and up the maids' staircase leading to the maids' bedrooms.

Well, after this there seemed to be constant walking and footsteps; at last we moved our living apartments downstairs to the servants' hall. But the footsteps seemed to pass by one in the daytime, but nothing could be seen. I am afraid it got me down, and very reluctantly we took another situation here at Brightlingsea, for my nerves got really strung up.

We were told on good authority that during this last war a soldier on guard down the drive was found in a faint whilst on guard duty and his rifle a few yards away. On recovering consciousness he said, "A lady in white had passed by him."

In the church of St Michael and All Angels standing in the park is a marble monument by J Edwards to Mrs Charlotte White, 1845. Charlotte was a member of the Smythe family; her effigy lies on a couch with two angels hovering near.

Another caretaker, Mr Gant, a very practical person, saw the shadow of a man: "Just the figure", he said: then it disappeared on a dim landing. It might have been the knight depicted on an old tapestry. He also saw the library door handle swing violently from side to side.

A house that must be nameless in a quaint riverside village not far from Colchester and built in the closing years of the last century is haunted by the ghost of 'Ben', who was a well-known Essex tradesman.

The occupiers were quite used to having 'Ben' as a permanent guest. The first occasion he made himself known was one night when there vas a noise like an echo or reverberation of the chiming door bells, followed by three knocks on a side door and knocking on a side window, but an inspection proved there was no one at the door or in the drive. The pekinese that usually barked and made a fuss when visitors arrived took no notice and walked out of the room as if no one was there. Old residents of the village said that 'Ben', as a young man, used to visit the maids in the servants' quarters, but not at this house, and three knocks was his signal.

On Boxing night, 1934, relatives were disturbed by someone walking up and down stairs as if in bare feet and asked if anyone had been up during the night. It was not the dog they said, but definitely the shuffling sound of bare feet. Quite often the door would open as if someone had entered; it was a spring latch and could not blow open. Things also used to disappear: a former cccupier was always saying that there was someone in and around the house and grounds and would 'phone the police, but her dogs never barked. It has been an ill-fated house for nearly all the owners have been unlucky in some way; two lost their money while living there.

Colchester has two ghosts related to the famous siege of 1648. An old house off Crouch Street is said to be haunted by a young Royalist soldier or, some say, a drummer boy. Unfortunately the tradition is vague and no reason for the manifestation is forthcoming. The house at the top of Headgate Court, Head Street (now offices, as are the surrounding buildings, some of which have been rebuilt) is said to have been visited ever since the surrender of the town by a cavalier or trooper, who in the still hours of the night may be heard parading in the grounds.

Edward S Knights tells in *Essex Folk* of a ghost that appeared to some purpose. Sheldrakes Farm, Latchingdon, was so named after its eccentric owner. When he died the inhabitants were disturbed by mysterious banging and rattling in one of the rooms. Someone saw old Sheldrake's ghost, apparently concerned with the hearthstone in the room. When the stone was raised, valuable papers and most of his savings were discovered. After this, Sheldrake's ghost, having achieved his object, did not appear again.

15th century Little Wakering Hall is said to have been haunted by a lady called Betty Bury who hanged herself in an attic after having been jilted by her lover. Betty is said to have rung the alarm bell that hangs on the roof, at least it is said to have been rung by mysterious means. Her ghost is supposed to be headless, as so many legendary ghosts are, and the detail was, no doubt, added to the tale in later years. Betty was also thought to haunt the lane leading to the house. Years ago people were afraid to go up it after dark and in autumn on misty nights her restive spirit haunts the Wick Meadow, as she creeps noiselessly along behind the Church between the Hall and Wakering Wick. The trees in Wick Meadow seem to shiver and shake when she is walking there even in high summer when there is no wind.

In recent years her ghost has walked along the village street and people have been startled to hear the rustle of her dress as she swishes by, but some years ago Mr Fulcher of High Street, Great Wakering, told me that he had never met anyone who had seen the ghost, only people who stated that their grandfather or someone they knew had seen her. He and his family used to jokingly cry up the attic stairs, "Betty, where are you? Come down, Betty."

In the second half of the 19th century servants sleeping in the west wing had their bedclothing pulled off in the night. A trap door led up to these rooms and it was found that a groom was playing a practical joke. However, horses at the big stables have been let out by some mysterious agency. The men would go in to breakfast and on their return find the horses were loose.

This is undoubtedly a folktale founded on fact, but the date when Betty lived at the Hall is not known. In Little Wakering Church there is a gravestone of Bradford Bury of the Hall, who died 10 July, 1675, aged 48; he was probably a near relative of Betty.

An old house and cottage in Rochford have an interesting legend connected with a haunted room. The story goes that at some unknown date, probably 300 years ago as parts of the house date from the 16th century, a gentleman and his young and ambitious wife lived in a small wooden house or cottage in East Street. The wife wished for a bigger and better house, so the husband built a new house on to the front of the cottage. The wife, still not satisfied with her lot, demanded more. At last the husband became so angry that he shut the lady up in a small room, almost a large cupboard, where she starved to death. It is said that the butler or servant used to bring food to the door of the room to tantalise her with its appetizing smell.

For years the room at the angle where the newer part of the house joins the original building was shut up and known as the haunted room. When the family occupying the house for many years wanted to make a bathroom over the haunted room the workmen had to get through the floor to put in the pipes. The ceiling of the haunted room is exceedingly low and the bathroom floor is lower than that of the other rooms on the upper floor.

Another tale is that the wife was shut in one of the attics and the small room was a priest hole.

The only record of anything supernatural is that one lady stayed but a short time in the older part of the house, because she said she could not stand the woman who came and stared at her at night. Her cat, as soon as it was taken there, ran away and was not seen again.

According to a report in the local press on Christmas Day, 1951, Mr B Murray of the Tower House Preparatory School, Little Burstead, otherwise known as Hope House, heard the ship's bell peal at noon while no one was in the house. A few days later he heard noises of 'walking about outside', but there was no one in sight. A piano played itself without anyone touching it. The manifestations, he declared, were authentic. The house is 300 years old and the legend is that a former occupier of nearby Stockwell Hall exercised his dogs in the school grounds.

16th century Stockwell Hall is locally known as Clock House as there is a clock in one of the gables. The figures on this clock are formed from blackened human bones, said to date from the time of the Civil War, but there is no proof of this and no tale to account for why these gruesome relics were used or how they were obtained.

Sometimes when a guest was having tea at Clatterford Hall, Fyfield, she would remark, "I thought we were alone, but I see you have another visitor." Her hostess, Mrs Challis, would assure her that they were alone. "But who was the old lady that crossed the room with a basket on her arm?", the guest would ask. Mrs Challis would answer, "It is only our ghost, she comes quite often." Who the ghost was or where she came from was not known [*Essex Weekly News* 23 May, 1952].

A lady and her mother lived for fourteen years in a house in Selbourne Road, Thundersley, but during the last four years a ghost in hobnail boots turned up and worried them so much that they moved house. It began when they heard footsteps at the back of the house and then someone walking about inside, but no one was there. Again and again the footsteps of someone in hobnail boots were heard, but nothing was disturbed and the doors always remained bolted. Later there were loud rappings on the walls and floors and one Sunday an unearthly scream was heard in the kitchen; it stopped when the door was opened [*Daily Mirror* 28 February, 1949].

At Shoeburyness is a small brick house dated 1673 known as Red House that has several stories told about it. Some say that the ghost of a girl who had cut her throat to spite her lover haunts the place, but the occupier in 1948, Mrs E L Phillips, said that she did not believe the story. She had lived there all her life, but had never seen anything, although they did hear all kinds of knocking noises and she had never been able to find out the reason, though she had gone up and down stairs at midnight many times to find out what made the sounds [*Southend Standard*

11 March, 1948]. When the tiles were removed in 1948 the attics saw the light of day for the first time since it was built. A four inch thick carpet of dust was found, a curtain of cobwebs and a swarm of the largest spiders the builders had ever seen. At the same time a wheelbarrow dislodged a stone in the garden path disclosing the shaft of an old well where the entrance to an underground tunnel leading to Shoebury Manor, a quarter mile away, is supposed to have been. The well was filled in with no attempt to solve the mystery.

16th century Hill Hall, Theydon Mount, once the seat of the Smith family, contains a room where seven brothers died 300 years ago. Blood stains are said to be still on the floor of a room known as the 'Brothers' Room' where this event is reputed to have occurred. During a sale this was the only room not opened to the public.

There is a tradition that in the 17th century a family of seven sons and one daughter lived in the Hall. The daughter formed an attachment with a man of whom her brothers did not approve. The brothers then one by one fought duels with the man and one by one were killed. The remorseful sister dressed herself in bridal attire and committed suicide. Since then Hill Hall has been haunted, the ghost appearing at midnight when a male owner of the Hall meets with a violent death: this has happened at least twice.

In August, 1948, a young lady staying at the Agricultural Camp at Theydon Mount was walking through the grounds when she saw what she thought was a ghost of a woman who appeared to be dressed as a bride. There was a note given at the foot of the account given in the *Essex Weekly News* of 20 August, 1948, that it was the young lady's first night there. Officials of the Camp had stayed up on several occasions to lay the ghost, but had not seen anything. The legend is believed by all, but there is no contemporary evidence to support it, only the persistence of the story over the years. It was commonly believed by those who have owned or worked in the house to be an 'unhappy house': in recent years it was a prison without bars for women.

Riffhams in Little Baddow, according to a village tradition, has a ghost of a recusant whose body, because of the lack of a Romish priest and rites, lay unburied for a long time in the room over the north porch [*Essex Review* January, 1934, No.169, Vol.XLIII].

Spains Hall, Finchingfield, once had a child ghost. In the first half of the 17th century William Kempe, the then owner of the mansion, voluntarily punished himself by imposing a vow of seven years' silence because of some rash words he had said. He kept the vow, although some dreadful consequences were the result. In the fifth year of his self-imposed punishment he was caught in a storm while returning from a business visit. Whilst sheltering in the old and eerie keep of Hedingham Castle he heard the voices of robbers in a room above plotting to raid Spains Hall. Kempe had with him his groom whom he had taught to understand him by signs and the man seemed to know there was danger.

The Blackwater was swollen with a cloud burst and, to get to Spains Hall, they had to cross the river. William would not speak although the danger was great. His servant begged him to return by a longer way, while he would swim his horse across the water and warn the household, even though he did not know what the danger was. Still

William would not speak. Instead, he wrote a message on a piece of paper and the groom struggled bravely through the floods to the Hall. By then the note was unreadable, the water having washed off the words. So all the able bodied men sallied forth to meet their master and the unknown danger.

While the house was unprotected the robbers arrived. They cared nothing for floods and had crossed the river, soon stripping the house of everything valuable and killing a little boy of 7 or 8 years old, a distant relative of the Kempes. The robbers were soon away in the darkness and were never discovered.

After this it was said that on stormy nights the spirit of the child haunted the wing of the house where he was murdered. No doubt after this terrible night everyone was nervy and so the tale grew that a small white clad figure could be dimly seen during storms. The wing where the murder happened was burnt down in Georgian times and the ghost is no longer seen.

Billericay still has several houses said to harbour ghosts. There are two ghost stories connected with the Cheyne Library, 118 High Street, which was rebuilt after being burnt down in 1956. One story is of an inhabitant who hanged himself in the cellars after his life savings had been stolen. Another later resident saw a girl going up the stairs in front of her and thought it was her daughter. However, as the girl should have been in bed, the mother went into the bedroom and found her daughter in bed where she had been for some time.

The 17th century house that had a projecting upper storey, which stood on the site of Billericay Post Office was haunted by a young lady in white. The house was 'extremely eerie and depressing with low ceilings and dark gloomy attics reached by a staircase with a gate at the bottom'; it was no doubt easy to imagine things.

A former tenant of St Aubyns, a 16th century house in Chapel Street, claimed that the house was haunted. In 1951, soon after Mr Richman had moved into St Aubyns, a visitor who was not at all imaginative in this respect was lying in bed after everyone was downstairs and she swore later that she was certain someone was in the room looking at her. At first she took no notice, as she thought Mr Richman's mother, who shared the room with her, had returned for some purpose or other. Anyway, there was no movement or sound, so she turned round to see who was there and the room was empty, except for herself. Mrs Richman had not been near.

In 1956 Mr Richman heard of two different experiences said to be some distance apart and not known by the second person to have happened to the first till both were living elsewhere.

The first lived in St Aubyns during the first World War. It was not until fairly recently that she met a lady who used to live there between the wars who said that she was never so scared in her life as when she lived in this house. Asked why, she described exactly the same experience which the other lady had had years before.

It was 'just like someone with dragging footsteps and holding on to the wall for support coming from the front room door (not the front door a few feet beyond) along the main passage, then at right angles along the other passage towards the kitchen door' at which point the steps ceased. The lady who had lived there first said it also sounded as if the person was dragging something behind him. This happened on several occasions, but on one a little worse than usual. She was working in the kitchen when it happened and she could not help looking towards the glass door to the passage to see who was coming. No one did and the steps ceased as they always did. She was so frightened that she could not do anything until her husband arrived home from work, when she ran to meet him trembling and almost in tears. She and the other lady, with whom there was no collusion, both said the steps were not to be confused with those of neighbours on either side, which can be heard, but only faintly, at times, but were quite distinctly in the house itself.

The Richmans did not have this experience, but they often heard footsteps coming from the front door (not the front room as the other ladies) and sometimes heard the door open and close first. The steps came down the passage and then straight upstairs to the first floor. Once they used to go and look, but later they never bothered, but a male friend who frequently visited them made a point of seeing if there was anyone - but there never was.

Mr Richman and his mother also had a very curious experience in the kitchen one evening in 1956 about 10-11 p.m. Mr Richman arrived home to find his mother sitting looking intently at the wall opposite. She told him, "I'm just watching the shadow of a ghost!" and asked him to watch the walls after noting there was nothing cooking or boiling on the stove and no tea or other beverage on the table or elsewhere to cause any steam or vapour. After a moment or so they saw a hasty flash of a shadow, almost like that of steam, but without any continued existence as it would - have been from the shadow of steam from a kettle or other utensil.

Mr Richman laughingly remarked that it was the ghost of steam from a vessel carried from the old copper, where generations of women have worked. It was just a flash across the chimney breast (there was no fire), followed a few seconds later by the same on the next or inner wall. The shadow passed across a small mirror. Mother and son tried to repeat the shadow or reflection by means of various objects on the table. but without result. The curtains were drawn and the door was shut and bolted. The next 'shadow' flashed across the door and it was when yet another flash of the same shadow went across the fourth wall and across the white plate at the back of the gas stove, that Mr Richman remembered he had seen exactly the same thing at the same point on a number of occasions about that time of night, but had never really taken much notice of it. The same 'shadow' was repeated on each wall in turn several times as they watched, but since then it has not been seen.

The 400-year-old house, Hurlocks, High Street, Billericay, was also haunted. Its ruinous condition before it was demolished in 1958 made it easy to imagine ghostly inhabitants. Towards the end of the last century Miss E S Bayly spent a troubled night in the 'spare room' and more recently a ghost was seen looking out of a window when the house was unoccupied. Hurlocks was demolished in 1958, the site is now a supermarket.

The Hyde, Great Wigborough, is haunted by a ghost called Prudence. In the early 16th century she was thought to be a witch and was burnt at the stake. There is a place in the garden where it is thought she may have been killed. The dog does not like this spot. Prudence has spoken when a seance was held; she had a 16th century Essex accent and said, "I frightened you," referring to an occasion when a stone hit a window when there was no-one there to throw it. The house has been exorcised, but there have been other incidents. Nylons in the main lounge disappeared for no reason and three days later they reappeared in the same spot. When there was a firework party one night and the room was empty, there was the sound of a piano being played. The present occupiers are not worried; they feel that there are benign spirits walking about.

Eastbury House, Barking, is also reputed to be haunted. A lady who worked there told me that a door in the kitchen would open and close and no one came in. When she remarked on this fellow workers told her it often happened.

When a family moved temporarily from some old cottages near Prittlewell Priory to a nearby bungalow an old lady in Victorian costume appeared: the whole family saw her. They discovered she bore a resemblance to someone who had once occupied the cottage and they wondered if she would follow them back when they returned there.

The new owners of 400-year-old Clements Hall, Hawkwell, in 1965 jokingly pulled a friend's leg, saying the house was haunted, but the joke became a reality when footsteps were heard. Three members of the family heard them and apparently the dog did too, for he went to the panelling wagging his tail, so it appears to be a friendly ghost.

One house had a very definite ghost for years. An old Water Company house in Lower Crescent, Linford, was haunted for ten years by Nobby Barker, who used to live there and work at the Linford Pumping Station. He died in

1970. He was a friendly ghost and no one was afraid of him. His first appearance was when the lady of the house saw a man wearing a cap walk down the garden path, but on looking outside there was nobody there. Her husband said she must be imagining things, but on describing the ghost to workmen at the pumping station he found out that the ghost was Nobby. One day the wife was upstairs making beds and the dog barked downstairs. She heard someone come in the back door and a voice saying, "It's all right, Patsy, it's only me." When she came downstairs she found no one there. Nobby's ghost disappeared about the time that his widow died and did not come again. Maybe he had been looking for her in their old home.

St Mary the Virgin, Little Wakering

Strange tales from Runwell, Hadleigh and Billericay

What may be described as historical 'flash-back visions' have been experienced at Runwell Hall by a professional gentleman in the form of dreams that were remarkably vivid. The first night he spent at the Hall he had an 'odd' feeling and on the first Tuesday he slept there in March, 1951, he dreamt that he saw a man wearing long hose, short puffed breeches, roll top boots of rough leather, with half chain armour on the upper part of his body, with mailed arms. He had cuffs of azure and wore a hat with turned-up brim and a pale blue crown. In a guttural voice he exclaimed, "'Tis there, so Gavin said, in the green room."

This dream figure is thought to be George White, the nephew of Susannah Tonge, who was a lady in waiting to Mary I, while her husband was Clarencieux King of Arms. When he was killed in battle Mary gave the manor of Runwell to Susannah together with her emerald necklace, given to Mary by Philip of Spain. George White inherited the manor from Susannah (the family holding it until 1679), but he stole the necklace, putting the blame on a groom, the only man having access to Susannah's bedroom as he carried up and removed the footbath. George White's own father convicted the groom to be hanged and legend says that the groom said on the scaffold, "I did not steal the necklace, but I know who did. I know where it is hidden and if ever the thief attempts to get it I will haunt him through eternity. It is still believed by old Runwell people that the emeralds are still hidden at the Hall.

It is remarkable that this dream occurred every Tuesday and did so for four years - the 47th time on 6th March, 1956. As time went on the dream was amplified and became longer, so that my informant dreamt he was coming up Runwell Hill wearing the dress of between 1600 and 1700, with 40 or 50 people and a few wagons and horses. He and other persons cross the garden of the existing Hall and go through a door below ground level into a room lit with two lights, where a priest stands on a dias. The priest is wearing a white stole and a purple spade-shaped apron of the 14th century.

Strangely, when recently a 9-inch wall was broken down in the cellar a dais was found covered with a thick coating of dust and rubble, that corresponded with the position of that in the vision.

In the next part of the dream the man thought to be George White stands on a landing and points to a staircase that has long disappeared, although traces have been found. The gentleman in company with White walks down this stairway through the floor into the chapel (now a cellar), then they find their way back upstairs into his bedroom and the priest comes into the room. The name of the priest, Johannes Beche, came to him without being told and before he could connect it by other means with John Beche, the last Abbot of St John's Abbey, Colchester. The Abbot is holding his arm, which is almost severed, and he can hear the slow drip, drip of blood on the floor. Beche says, in French, "I have passed this way many times, now for the last time in flesh and blood, but in spirit for ever."

It is rumoured that John Beche took refuge and was hidden at Runwell Hall in 1536 at the Suppression of the

Monasteries and he was subsequently arrested, taken away and executed very barbarously, with the Abbots of Reading and Glastonbury. Susannah Tonge is said to have been a Protestant and had a chapel at the Hall; Beche may have officiated there, as he is thought to have had Protestant sympathies.

Runwell Hall was substantially rebuilt in 1824, but is basically 16th century. It is now an hotel.

¶¶¶¶

In an ancient cottage in High Street, Hadleigh, now demolished, Mrs Martha Hemmings had many unusual experiences. The cottage, originally stables connected with the nearby Castle Inn when it was a coaching house, was converted into Jim's Café and the Hemmings lived over it. Several apparitions were seen and the cottage also had an unseen presence that often made itself felt. Previous occupants also had uncanny experiences.

When Mrs Hemmings first saw the café it was in a very bad condition, but a man working in the kitchen seemed to be surrounded by coloured lights and she had what she described as a happy, holy feeling and in intense desire, despite its bad state of repair, to take the place. When she was away from it she felt quite different, but as soon as she returned she had no desire to leave and felt she had to be there. Mrs Hemmings, a vivacious person, may be said to be psychic. She is entirely convinced of her adventures and no one doubts her.

The cottage stood not far from the lane leading to Hadleigh Castle and Mrs Hemmings said that when she visited the Castle, at the gate to the footpath to Leigh, a voice said to her, "I belong here".

Shortly after they came to Hadleigh Mrs Hemmings was in the garden at the rear of the cottage when she felt as if she was lifted up or floating. Everything had a rosy glow. She felt a holy atmosphere and, looking up at the cottage, she saw standing at an upstairs window the figure of a thin old woman with piercing black eyes, holding a stick and dressed in old-fashioned clothes - a brown skirt, black apron and a deep purple blouse, with big leg-of-mutton sleeves. When she gave a description of this figure to an old inhabitant of Hadleigh, he said it resembled a relation of his who had lived in the cottage seventy years previously.

One Sunday night early in 1956 Mrs Hemmings was sitting upstairs and looking from one of the front windows she saw, reflected in the windows of the empty house opposite, her husband working in the café and behind him the apparition of a very dark, slim, young lady wearing a big hat and an old-fashioned grey costume with a high neck. With her was a little boy of about 12 years old wearing what appeared to be knee breeches and a Norfolk jacket and she could also seen the top part only of a white horse. The figures were transparent and her husband moved through them as he worked in the café. This phenomenon lasted about an hour; she saw it on one other occasion - also on a Sunday.

Twice in the same week she had the same strange dream in which the boy and the white horse appeared. In this dream the horse rushed madly to attack her, with glaring eyes and foaming at the mouth. Then she noticed the boy at her side and, looking round, she found she was standing before an antique shop and, putting her hand behind her, she took out of the shop window a brass statue of a knight in armour with a black cross on his shield and another on top of his helmet. This she aimed at the horse and it at once drew back.

Mrs Hemmings always referred to the ghost whose 'presence' she felt in the house as 'Annie' and then she discovered that a lady named Annie B--- did live in the cottage many years ago; it may be her ghost that she felt and has seen with the boy and the horse.

Mr Hemmings did not actually see anything, but had strange happenings. Articles mysteriously disappeared in the café and both husband and wife have seen the old fashioned latch on the upstairs door move up and down and heard it click when no one was there and there was no wind. Sometimes the door slowly opened and the air became suddenly chill.

One day when a customer was in the café Mr Hemmings was lifting a jug of hot water and holding a tea cloth over it when the cloth was snatched away and disappeared completely. A thorough search was made, but it was not found; later it turned up neatly rolled in a ball inside the jug he had been using during the day and where it certainly had not been when they were looking. Another time an apron was snatched from his arm and later reappeared behind the gas stove. A newspaper disappeared one morning and reappeared late in the afternoon in its original position.

The Hemmings' pet cat had two kittens. On the third day after their birth Mr Hemmings was in the room with the cat and kittens when there was a sudden uncanny cold draught in the room; the cat evidently sensed some thing for it spat and backed into its basket. Mr Hemmings was much affected by the evil feelings and had goose-flesh all over him as he went upstairs. Shortly after this the cat was taken ill and the kittens died, although no obvious connection can be made. The cat would never go upstairs and this, they thought, was because of the ghost.

One day Mr Hemmings went across the road for something, leaving a customer in the shop. This man knew that Mrs Hemmings was out and no one besides himself was in the building, but he heard footsteps cross the kitchen and the sounds of cups being placed in the sink. On Mr Hemmings' return he told him what he had heard and Mr Hemmings confirmed that they were the only people in the place, but when he looked in the sink he found some dirty cups in it that he had certainly not put there!

Spoons and other articles were sometimes snatched from their hands, but the customers assumed that they fell. Early in 1957 three half-pennies jumped out of the till, customers seeing it happen.

A medium sent a message that Mrs Hemmings would put a plaque on the wall. Shortly after that, some floor boards being removed, a shield-like plaque was found as the medium had described with 'God is Love' inscribed on it. It was hung on a beam in the café. A hymn written by a child was also found, covered with dust.

In June, 1956, Mrs Hemmings said that, when it was getting dark, she had seen a formless shadow in the corner of the café that was once the living room of the cottage. The shadow moved and altered as if it was becoming a shape. She could see the beginnings of eyes. Chairs were heard to creak as if someone was sitting in them. The couple said that the atmosphere was weird and uncanny at dusk. One evening Mr Hemmings jokingly said at supper time, "There you are, there's a chair for Annie and another for her companion," and set two extra chairs before he went into the kitchen. Shortly afterwards Mrs Hemmings saw a shadow on the wall that grew in intensity; it seemed to come off the wall and towards her, appearing to have eyes shining in the dusk; Mrs Hemmings was alarmed this time, although some what inured to these manifestations. "Annie, don't frighten me," she said and called for her husband, but the phenomenon had disappeared before he came. At this time they heard many strange noises and knocking. Three weeks afterwards Mrs Hemmings received a great shock on hearing of the death of someone in her family and the shadowy form was not seen thenceafter.

Most of the customers believed in the ghost, but Mrs Hemmings was not depressed, as she said it was a lucky house, bringing good fortune.

¶¶¶

The beautiful Georgian house, Burghstead Lodge, High Street, Billericay, has a spine-chilling tale told of a haunted bedroom at the back of the building (southwest room, first floor). The story is recounted by J A Sparvel-Bayly, who lived there in the late 70s and early 80s of the last century in *The Silent Lady, or an Essex Mystery*. He tells how an old retainer in the 19th century was engaged to be night nurse to a young, unknown gentleman at Burghstead Lodge. He was in a critical condition and was not to be spoken to unless necessary. The house, let to a non-resident nobleman and lived in by members of his family, had little to do with local tradesmen.

On the first night, as the nurse sat by the smouldering

log fire in the huge fireplace, there were no sounds but the meaning of the wind. At midnight the patient breathed heavily and seemed uneasy and the nurse was surprised to see a lady in a green silk gown with a black veil over her bonnet sitting by the bedhead. The nurse was unalarmed and curtsied and moved towards the bed. However, the lady motioned her to be seated, so the nurse sat and wondered how and when the lady had come in. It was cold and late for a visitor and she had been told that no visitors came. The lady sat watching the patient and repulsed the nurse when she approached the bed to help the patient, who was very uneasy. At last the nurse closed her eyes for a moment - the lady had disappeared and the patient was easier.

The following night was stormy with crispy sleet hissing on the window, the wind moaned down the spacious chimney and a distant door banged in the wind. The nurse felt uneasy and somewhat creepy and was thinking that she would give up her engagement, when the heavy breathing of her patient made her look up to see the lady in the green gown again seated by his bed.

The nurse thought she must be an inmate of the house, as her dress, the very low bodiced summer costume of the period, was quite unsuitable for the inclement weather. When the nurse rose to go to the bed she waved her back. The patient's agitation, however, so increased that the nurse did approach the bed in spite of the lady's gestures. The lady drew her veil across her face and retired to the window. The patient appeared in agony, with drops of perspiration rolling down his face, while his eyes followed the lady in her glittering gown and he repulsed all the nurse's offers of help. So she sat down again by the fire and the lady returned to the bed side. The nurse could not remember taking her eyes off the lady, but, as before, she was gone and the patient was easier.

The nurse told the physician in the morning that she could not carry on. He appeared surprised when told about the lady in green and asked the nurse to resume duty for that night, which she agreed to do.

That night she was determined to watch for the lady, but her vigilance was defeated. Weary with watching she raised her head yawning with fatigue and there, with lavishly displayed shoulders, was the lady. The nurse felt awestruck and when she approached the bed the lady retreated. The young man was cold with terror, his eyes straining from their sockets unconscious of everything but the mysterious lady. Nurse thought he was dying and was going for assistance, when the lady moved to the bed and bent over the dying man, then moving to the door. The nurse had one hand on the door latch and with the other she tried to raise the lady's veil, but nurse fell senseless to the floor for a death's head filled the large oldfashioned bonnet. A horrid laugh rang out, the lady disappeared and nurse knew no more. The next morning the nurse was found cold and numb on the floor and the patient appeared to have been dead for many hours.

The mysterious young man was buried in the parish church with a lavish funeral. A gentleman whose features bore a striking resemblance to the effigy upon the coin of the realm and a London physician alone followed the body to the grave. A plain and exquisite tablet was placed in the church a year afterwards bearing the words, "Charles Leroy died 29 February, 18--. Remember".

Poor nurse died three months after her dreadful ordeal

and the gloomy chamber was said to have a strange feeling of awe and coldness by whoever occupied it afterwards, although nothing was ever seen or heard to alarm the weakest nerves.

This story, although a good yarn, appears to be a mixture of fact and fiction. There is no tablet on the walls of the parish church, which at that time must have been St Mary Magdalen, Great Burstead, unless after 1844, when Billericay became a separate parish. At Great Burstead there is a tablet to a certain George Fitzgeorge of royal birth who was drowned in a pond near his school in Billericay High Street.

Mr Sparvel-Bayly used to point out the haunted room to visitors (especially young ladies), but his daughter said that she and her sisters never saw anything unusual, even when they slept in the room, but then Mr Bayly did say that nothing was there to alarm the weakest nerves.

The shrubbery of Burghstead Lodge, running along the Brentwood Road, part still exists, was said to be haunted by the ghost of a 'White Lady'. In later years a cook/housekeeper reported ghostly happenings in the basement and in 1958 two children exploring the house reported that there was a 'very nice lady' on the top floor, when in fact there was no one there.

Haunted inns

Mostly the only spirits that inns, however old, harbour are those in bottles, but Essex has a number of inns that are haunted, or reputed to be so.

The fine coaching inn, the Golden Fleece, in Brook Street, South Weald, is a suitable abode for a ghost for it is 500 years old. One evening about thirty years ago a lady was alone in an upstairs room, known as the coffee room, when she happened to look into a mirror. There she perceived the reflection of a monk with folded arms standing behind her. She turned round quickly, but there was no monk there and she was the only person in the room. Again she looked into the mirror, thinking she had been mistaken, but there was the monk still gravely regarding her. This was too much for the lady, who fled screaming downstairs. The Golden Fleece is said to have originally been St Peter's Priory, but there is no record of such a religious house. Weald Hall, not far away, belonged to the Abbey of Waltham, so there could be a connection between this and the spectral monk.

At the 400-years-old Star Inn at Ingatestone, standing nearly in the churchyard, there have been mysterious happenings. In 1956 two sisters refused to sleep at the inn any more because of the uncanny things that occurred there; they were too frightened to sleep in the front bedroom at night. Lights have been seen in the room by neighbours, but no one had turned them on. One night in 1955 one sister turned off the light and shut the door of the room; the next morning the lights were on and the door open. There was said to be something strange about the room. One day a main door in the Star swung open three times, but there was no draught and the door was properly latched. Carved on a beam over the fireplace are the initials 'G E M' and the date 16 [the next figure is not readable] 2. The beam was discovered when renovations were made. It is roughly hewn and rotten, so it was plastered over except for the inscription.

The old Green Man at Leytonstone, demolished in the 1920s, had a haunted room, but there does not seem to be any authentic record of a ghostly visitation, yet no servant would willingly enter the room alone. Being an inn frequented by highwaymen it was, no doubt, a story set about by these gentlemen and kindred souls, who wished for a place where they could be secure from interference and to which the superstitious folk of the time would give a wide berth and attribute any noises to the supernatural

There are well-attested reports of the haunting of another Essex inn, the three centuries old King's Head at Maldon. A man and woman spent Christmas, 1946, here and their nights were disturbed by a man's footsteps running up and down stairs and across the hall all night. Later a young man said that on two occasions, on going to the toilet during the night, he was unable to open the door to get out again; it seemed to be held against him by someone on the other side, the door opening inwards. After exerting all his force he got it open. He could see no one, but heard a man's footsteps hurrying away before him on a long strip of landing and go downstairs. This same lavatory door has sometimes been jammed from within by a large ashtray on the floor. The window is upstairs and very small, so how did it get there? When some flooring was taken up at this inn a pile of human bones was found. It was considered to have been a plague pit, but the churchyard is opposite and a possible explanation is that a bad landlord murdered his guests in times past.

At the Swan, Rayne, a high windowless chamber at the rear of the house is said to be haunted by a weaving woman who hanged herself from a beam of her loom.

Ghostly noises are supposed to have been heard at the 17th century White Horse at Great Baddow, which has been an inn for centuries. Many years ago a murder is said to have taken place there five days before Christmas. On 20th December, 1946, sounds, as of someone walking down the attic stairs, woke up the landlord, but nothing was out of place. The same thing had happened two years previously. Until 1947 the attic door was sealed by wallpaper; this door is about three feet high and a foot wide.

The centuries old Spotted Dog that stood in Tindal Street, Chelmsford, until the new shopping centre, was built had a bedroom with no door or window and no one, as far as is known, had been in it for 50 years or more. This room was between two other bedrooms and was kept sealed. The story goes that, many years ago, a man was knifed to death in mistake for another person while he was in the room; after this the room was sealed up. At Christmas time there were often strange tappings inside, as if someone wanted to get out. Sometimes doors and windows rattled when there was no wind at all and once a bowl in one of the bedrooms slipped off a table for no apparent reason.

In 1963 a ghost was reported at the Swan, Brentwood. Religious plates on the wall tumbled down, lights were switched on and chairs dragged about. A door rattled as if someone was in a hurry, but on opening it no one was there. Unexplained draughts and noises were felt and heard. The ghost was thought to be the 19 year old martyr, William Hunter, who spent his last hours at the Swan before being burnt at the stake in 1555.

One ghost from an old house took over a new house; when the Beehive at Great Waltham was rebuilt the ghost, an Elizabethan known as Old Ruffy, is reported to have caused glasses to disintegrate during the night. Occasionally glasses have been shattered while being held. Spiritualists said the glass-breaking was caused by a spirit trying to attract attention.

At the 17th century Fox at Mashbury the sounds of a phantom coach have been heard and an invisible 'customer' also enters the bar - to the discomfiture of the landlord's dog! The front door leading into the public bar has rattled as if a flesh and blood customer has entered, but each time there has been no one. Once when the door rattled it seemed as if someone had come into the room and the landlord went at once to the bar. He was aware, he said, of someone or something passing him, as if a piece of muslin or a cobweb was being drawn across his face, but there was no one to be seen. A Pyrex dish placed in safety in a cupboard shelf was found smashed to pieces. On more than one occasion he heard the jingle of harness and noise of heavy wheels of a horse drawn coach crunching the gravel as they turned round in the forecourt of the Fox; he rushed to the door and looked out. Apart from the rhythmic sounds of horses' hooves pulling away a phantom coach there was nothing. His dog has frequently suddenly stopped dead in his tracks and with teeth bared and hair bristling has apparently seen something or someone unseen to the landlord. Previously the landlord had been sceptical of such things, but this convinced him.

At the 16th century Black Horse at White Roding a ghost a few years ago sometimes played weird and beautiful music on a piano in the bar. The landlord, who firmly believed in the ghost, crept downstairs, but when he opened the door the music ceased and the piano lid in the deserted bar was closed. Doors have been opened and shut at night by some invisible hand and bottles opened by the same mysterious means. Legend says the ghost of a cavalier who was brutally murdered haunts the district. The landlord got rid of the piano, but they have not got rid of whatever it is - they still hear something from time to time, who they call George.

A cottage at East Mersea, formerly the Ship Inn, was said to be haunted by a smuggler's sweetheart who had been murdered there. The family who lived there were quite used to meeting her. The old cottage was burnt down about 60 years ago and a new house built on the site. Later another cottage was built nearby, which is also supposed to be haunted. This story is most likely connected with a seance held on Mersea Island that is mentioned in *Travels in East Anglia* by F V Morley.

Thatched roofed and vine-covered, the Sutton Arms at Little Hallingbury is said to be more than 500 years old. It owes its sign to the family of Thomas Sutton, founder of Charterhouse School, who was a landowner hereabouts. Legend has it that one of the Suttons fell for a pretty serving-maid at the pub, but he was rejected so he strangled her. Now forever he walks the creaking boards of the inn seeking to make it up to her with a bag of gold.

He has not been seen by recent landlords, but things sometimes move unaccountably.

At Harwich's early 16th century Three Cups, Nelson is said to have stayed with Lady Hamilton and her ghost was seen by the proprietor's wife and daughter during World War II, who had used the room where Emma had slept. After the war the brewers knocked down the wall and altered the room: the ghost has not been seen since.

Some years ago there were some most unusual occurrences at the Maybush at Great Oakley. Strange unaccountable noises were regularly heard in the silent hours of the night; the peculiar sound of marbles rolling along the timbers of an upstairs room as well as the un explained sounds of falling objects. Also at the time there were rumoured stories of a phantom oriental lady who chose to visit the Maybush at night. Seances were held in the bar to establish some reason for the ghostly disturbances that allegedly had taken place in a dwelling whose occupants included young persons.

The Tarpot, South Benfleet, which is a modern house, has a ghostly barman. The man collapsed and died there in 1946 and has been seen, complete with white button hole, on various occasions. He was seen very clearly by D D Parson, according to a report in the *News Review,* December, 1968. Mr Parson said, "But no-one need be frightened of him - he's a very friendly fellow."

The World's End inn near Tilbury Fort, has, according to a landlord, a friendly ghost. The inn was probably the haunt of highwayman Nick Nevinson, known as Swift Nick, and it may be his ghost that haunts the pub. The landlord's wife saw the ghost leaning over a cot. Sometimes it has reactivated fires that have been out for hours

- or even days. On Christmas Eve, 1982, it excelled itself and the fire alarm sounded at 3 a.m.: the landlord and his wife came down to find a blazing fire in the hearth where there had been nothing but ashes a few hours before.

Rayleigh Lodge has a customer who turns up after the last bell has rung. The manager, Bryan Matthews, said, "To be honest I was frightened as it brushed past me up the stairs, the structural work seems to have disturbed it." Rayleigh Lodge was once a hunting lodge in Henry VIll's time and the ghost, according to local belief, os that of a girl who became pregnant by the Lord of the Manor, who threw herself into a pond adjacent to the pub. The apparition, traditionally supposed to wear a dark trailing dress, moves around the bar and first made her appearance in 1973. The manager's wife felt cold fingers touch her shoulder one night. Mr Matthews' samoyed dog refused to sleep in the bar and settled outside his master's bedroom. Three attempts to exorcise the ghost have had no effect.

The 18th century Jolly Waggoners at Manuden has an active invisible ghost, who has wakened guests with ice-cold hands pulling at their arms. Lights have been switched on and off and articles moved, but, although strange noises have been heard and footprints seen, no apparition has appeared. The Yew Tree, also in Manuden, beats the Waggoners, as it boasts two ghosts, both of which have been seen.

Local people say that a ghostly monk, probably from Earl's Colne Priory, has appeared in the bar of the ancient Castle Inn in the village several times.

The ghost of a publican who was shot in the 19th century in the backyard of the Ship Inn, West Thurrock, is said to haunt the place.

Mysterious happenings in many places

Of the famous Borley Rectory it is hardly necessary to add to the store of information already published, but when some people took a piece of stone from the site and later at a spiritualist meeting handed it to the medium, she said she experienced a terrible feeling of danger. "There has been a murder," she declared. Afterwards they were warned that they had done a dangerous thing, for an evil spirit could have been released.

Mrs Owen, widow of Canon Owen, told me of a ghost that haunted Bradwell Lodge, formerly the Rectory, at Bradwell-juxta-Mare. She said that when her husband succeeded his brother at Bradwell she was told there was a ghost - the butler of a former rector. He tried to commit suicide in a small room upstairs and came down and died in the library. Her nieces said they had never seen him, but had heard him walking about. They did not use the little room as a rule, but Mrs Owen put a young housemaid into it and the next morning she said she could not sleep there again. Mrs Owen's father-in-law came to Bradwell in 1870, so the ghost must ante-date that. It is also said that the ghost of a child has been seen at Bradwell Lodge. The Lodge is a charming residence of two main parts - the Elizabethan North Wing, with its long oak-beamed library, dating from 1520, and the South Wing, added 1781-6, a wonderful example of Georgian architecture by John Johnson. The room mentioned by Mrs Owen, the Bishop's Room, is still known as the haunted room.

When the Misses Shaw, two grand-daughters of Canon Bateman, who was rector of Southchurch from 1873 to 1893, paid a visit to Southend on Sea in 1933 they told the then rector, Canon M Elphinstone, that when Canon Bateman first came to the Rectory it was reputed to be haunted by a rector of long ago who, for his 'greed of gain' was doomed after death to roam the passages at night [*Southend Observer* 11 November, 1933].

There was a story that a monk haunted one bedroom in the old Ashingdon Rectory, but no one had seen or heard of him in later years. It was not an ancient house, being only a hundred years old; it has now been demolished and a new rectory built on the site.

Ghostly footsteps were heard in 17th century Sutton Rectory, just outside Southend. Some years ago a rector told how, soon after the family arrived at the rectory, his two daughters, one aged 21 and the other 12, had mentioned strange noises in their bedroom, but were told that they were due to mice. The elder daughter was somnambulist. One moonlight night he was awakened by noises and, thinking his daughter was on the move, he hurriedly slipped on a dressing gown and stationed himself at the head of the stairs to prevent her falling down. He saw no one in the corridor, but distinctly heard someone walking there. The footsteps became louder and came towards him. They came right up to him and passed on through him. His hair began to rise and he fled back to bed. Mrs V Tabor, JP, who lived in the building for twenty years, said, "I never talked about it, but it is a fact that strange things did happen at night in a certain bedroom in the house. A number of people experienced the presence of a ghost when they stayed overnight in this room" [*Essex Weekly* 29

November, 1963].

When Fred Pope of South Benfleet was engaged in demolishing the rectory in 1963 he told of a dark, smoky, shadowy figure, shapeless except for its head, which moved soundlessly downstairs and along passages, only to disappear, always in the same dark corner of the cellar. All the workmen were said to have seen it and Fred declared it followed him home and frightened his wife half to death. It only appeared during the day. Doors were seen to open and shut and a stack of wood piled in one room was mysteriously moved by no one to another. I visited the house when it was being pulled down on a foggy November evening as dusk as falling, but I did not see the strange moving shadow that the men said they had been seeing. There were 21 rooms and four staircases, including a spiral staircase leading from the first floor to the attic. It was all very sad and melancholy in the early winter dusk.

A luminous spectre was seen in the lovely old Stuart manor house of Fremnells, Downham, that was destroyed in 1954 when the Hanningfield Reservoir was built. In 1951 a gentleman who often stayed in this historic house woke up for some reason in the dead of night and saw the ghost - a shape all shimmering with light - no face could be seen, but he had the impression that it was the ghost of a man. He had no doubt concerning its reality; it was almost like something aglow with phosphorescence. Seeing the spectre approach he switched on his bedside lamp. There was no one there and when he turned off the light the thing had vanished. This happened twice in just over a month. Fremnells, a gracious house with its red brick gabled front mellowed by time, was once the home of Benjamin Disbrow, whose mother was one of Oliver

Cromwell's sisters. It is said hat the whole of the Disbrow family died of smallpox at Fremnells in the early 19th century. There is also a legend that Dick Turpin rode his horse up the stairs and stabled it in one of the attics which had once been a chapel. Mrs Kirk, wife of the late occupier, could remember a manger in the attic. Many of the former residents of Fremnells lie in St Margarets, Downham, where their monuments can be seen.

There are several stories, ghostly and otherwise, told of the beautiful old mansion of Porters at Southend on Sea, now owned by the Corporation and used as the Mayor's Parlour. There have been two experiences in the house within recent years of ghostly manifestations. A young man working alone late one night in an upper room was checking a letter when he felt a tap on his shoulder. He did not dare turn round, the tap was repeated, he dropped the letter and, screwing up his courage, turned round - there was no one there! Another man, also working late upstairs, heard someone cross the landing below. He assumed it was the Mace Bearer until he found that no one else had been in the house at the time.

Oliver Cromwell is reputed to have slept one night at Porters during the Civil War. Whether or not this is true, it is known from the records that Cromwellian soldiers came to Porters and the family shut themselves in an upstairs room, where the family silver and plate were kept; this was known as the Record Room - its stout door still exists. The silver and other valuables were let down through a trap door into the kitchen and thence was taken to a pond at the bottom of the grounds, where it was hidden. The pond is still there.

Porters was built about the beginning of the 17th

century. On the right hand side of the chimney in the Oak Room is a secret room big enough to conceal two or three persons, but it has been sealed up for some years. There is also a tradition of a secret passage leading to the sea. A former owner had spoken to people who claimed to have played in it as children, but it might have been a culvert.

At the 14th century manor house of Southchurch Hall, Southend, footsteps have been heard walking across the hall, as if someone was sweeping.

Although, perhaps, not strictly a ghost story the experience of a Methodist minister at Little Oakley is distinctly uncanny. He was visiting the farmhouse of Mr Clothier in the autumn when it was getting dusk. The servant showed him into an old-fashioned room, where a lamp stood in the middle of a table covered with a velvet cloth. The servant lit the lamp, which had an octagonal glass container and a large red globe surrounding the light. When she had left the room the minister saw a clear picture form on the glass globe of the lamp of a four poster bed in a bedroom. On the bed was a woman whose features could be clearly seen. She appeared to be ill. A man approached the bed and lifted up the bedclothes over the woman's face. The vision lasted about a minute and the minister was spellbound. When the vision disappeared he examined the globe to see if there was a design or picture on it, but it was entirely plain.

When Mr Clothier came in the minister at once recognised him as the man he had seen in the lamp. They talked about the chapel and its services quite normally, but the minister was very uneasy and kept looking at the lamp, although nothing else appeared. Presently the servant asked for Mr Clothier, who excused himself and left the room.

Later the servant returned and told him that Mr Clothier's wife had died and her master asked if he would go up to the bedroom. There, exactly as he had seen in the lamp, was the four poster and the woman whose features he recognised and, as he entered the room, the husband lifted the sheet over his dead wife's face. This could have been an instance of the power of dying people to 'project' themselves on to the vision of others, although the receiver was a complete stranger - or it could have been self-hypnosis brought about by staring at the red lamp.[1]

Danbury has three ancient houses not far from the church that are haunted by poltergeists, the sort of spirit who throws things about, stumps on the stairs and pulls the bedclothes off, but for various reasons the properties cannot be named. At one, maids will not stay: at the top of the stairs there is a 'cold spot'. The pet dog of the family was found one day on the landing unable to move and quite numb with terror. The unfortunate animal nearly died and the vet said it was entirely due to sheer fright. Undoubtedly the dog had seen or felt some terribly evil thing. At another house the tenants had to leave as the poltergeist made their lives unbearable, but later tenants do not seem to have been troubled.

A Stansted Mountfitchet poltergeist became news in 1947 when George Thurston and his wife left the place after they had lived there for thirty years. When the children were young they were taken out of their beds and parked under the table, lamps were put out and torches turned on and locked doors opened. When airmen spent a night in there all slept peacefully except Sgt Schilling, who said he saw vapour rise and come towards him, causing a peculiar, but very powerful, sensation.

Strange knockings and rappings are firmly believed by some Essex folk to be signs foretelling a death in the family. My mother and her sister were sitting one evening in our lonely farmhouse on the edge of the marshes when they both heard a knock at the back door. On going to the door there was no sign of any visitor. This, my mother thought, foretold the death of an uncle that occurred shortly afterwards. There may have been some explanation of this knock, but there does not seem to be any for another uncanny happening, this time at West Mersea. Mother's 10-year old sister had died and she was lying in her coffin downstairs. Mother and my grandmother, who was always called 'Ma' by her daughters, were alone in the house. They were making beds upstairs when they both distinctly heard a voice call, "Ma," yet there was only the dead girl downstairs.

Just before Broomfield village is reached stands a very old residence called Well House, from a well that is beneath it. In 1772 Thomas Dixon came to live here; he was a widower and later his son, Robert, also a widower, joined him. On Easter Tuesday, 1785, Thomas died early in the morning and Robert died a few hours after. The double funeral was on 10 April in Broomfield Cemetery. At midnight, just previous to Thomas's death, the doctor and nurse were watching by his bedside when they heard a knock at the door. The nurse opened it, finding nothing. This happened a second time and the nurse could discover no one. The third time they were disturbed the doctor swore and the nurse looked up and down the landing, but no one was to be seen and there was nothing to account for the knocking. They never did find out the reason, but said it was 'knocking for the dead' [*Essex Review, Vol* XXLX,

No.16, October, 1920].

Another house in Broomfield, 16th century Priors was, in the last century, reputed to be haunted and for this reason was uninhabited for a long time. One room is still known as the Haunted Room. Priors is so named because it formerly belonged to Blackmore Priory.

Mrs ☺, who lives at Benfleet, had a very queer experience a few years ago in her modern house. One night as she was going up the stairs to bed she heard a key turn in the lock of the front door. She turned - who could it be? The door did not open, so she went down and opened it - no one there. It was thought that someone had made a mistake and come to the wrong house or was playing a joke and had run away before the door was opened. Shortly after this Mrs ☺ went on holiday and, on her return, was told that nearly every night while she was away the lock turned as if a key was in it, but however quick they were, when the door opened there was nobody to be seen. The lock was taken to pieces to find out if there was any reason for the strange happenings, but there was nothing to account for them and it happened on nights that were perfectly still and windless. For a time it stopped, then it began again. Mrs ☺ believed it to be the spirit of her husband and asked for Masses to be said for his soul. After that it ceased.

Mrs ¶ often used to see the old lady living next door pottering about the garden followed by a pale, wishy-washy looking little boy of about seven years old wearing butcher blue trousers and concluded he was her grandson. One day the old lady brought back one of the children's balls that had gone over the fence and in course of conversation the little boy was mentioned. There was no child living in the house Mrs ¶ was told. "But I often see a little boy following you round the garden," said Mrs ¶ and described the child. "Well, you have never seen him with me," replied the old lady. There had been such a boy, but he had died in hospital on the day his parents had moved into the house.

A queer story is told of a bride-to-be at an Essex house that seems to be Langleys, Great Waltham, in 1623 [*Essex Review*, Vol XXVII, July, 1918]. Sir Charles Lee's first wife died when their daughter was born and the girl was brought up by her aunt, Lady Everard. When she was of marriageable age a match was concluded for her with Sir William Perkins, but one Thursday night she thought she saw a light in her room after she was in bed. She called the maid who said there was no candle and the fire was out, so, thinking it was a dream, she went to sleep again. About 2 o'clock in the morning she was reawakened, this time by the apparition of a little woman between the curtain and the pillow, who said she was her mother, that she was very happy and that, by twelve of the clock that day, she should be with her. The young lady then rose, dressed and went into her room and did not come out until nine, when she gave her aunt a letter for her father, told her what had happened and desired the letter might be sent as soon as she was dead.

The aunt thought she was mad and sent for a physician and surgeon from Chelmsford, who both came at once, but failed to find anything wrong with the girl. However, they let blood and she patiently let them do as they wished, then asked for the chaplain to read prayers. Afterwards she took her guitar and psalm book and played and sang so well that her music master admired it. At twelve she rose and seated herself in a big chair, breathed deeply and immediately expired, becoming cold so quickly that the physician and surgeon were amazed.

At Great Codham Hall, a 14th century house at Wethersfield, a son appeared to his mother on the morning he died in a duel. On 28th February, 1712/13, Henry Pyne was killed by Sir Theophilus Biddulph at Chelsea. On the same morning his mother waking in broad daylight saw his bloody apparition. She woke up her husband, who tried to persuade her that it was but a vivid dream, but she went downstairs and turned into a room where she saw the figure again. After breakfast, as she left the house to go into the garden, a servant rode up with the sad news.

Springfield Place, near Chelmsford, was originally occupied by a branch of the Petre family. By 1864 it became noted for the apparition of a dwarf-like figure that appeared at various times and, in later years, in the panelled Blue Room. In 1946, when the house was requisitioned as a girls' hostel, it was reported that two of the girls sleeping on the top floor awoke in fright, complaining that something uncanny had touched their faces. There were also other strange happenings, including the unaccountable falling of various articles [*Essex Weekly News,* February, 1946 & 13 June, 1952].

Many gabled Ingatestone Hall, built for Sir William Petre in 1548, has two traditional ghosts. Sir William was a remarkable man; he acted as one of the Royal Commissioners for the Dissolution of the Monasteries and bought Ingatestone Manor, which had belonged to the nunnery at Barking, from the Crown. He served Henry VIII, Edward IV, and Mary, surviving all the political and religious upheavals to entertain Elizabeth at Ingatestone in

1561. The tradition persisted in 1851 that his ghost haunted the turret in the corner of the inner court that leads to the upper rooms and it is said to have been felt by the caretaker. A ghost is said to flit up and down the lovely lime walk: perhaps it is that of Lady Katherine Grey, younger sister of Lady Jane, who married the Earl of Hertford without Elizabeth's consent. She was in Sir William's custody for two years and probably resided at Ingatestone.

The mid-18th century mansion of Hutton Hall, near Brentwood, has a ghostly grey lady; she haunts the panelled bedroom on the first floor. I cannot discover that anyone has seen her recently or the other ghostly lady said to be seen in Hanging Hill Lane, Hutton, and the reason for their haunting has been long forgotten.

Many ancient houses have a room that is traditionally said to be haunted. This is so at the 15th century red brick mansion of Faulkbourne Hall that is almost a castle. A room known as the Bishop's Room, which had a priests' hole (now blocked up), has always been said to be haunted. It has been assumed that there must have been access from the priests' hole to a second room where the priest could hide during times of religious persecution. Probably this background made it known as the haunted room. Certainly some members of the owner's family in past years would never sleep in it, yet there is no definite story.

A ghostly presence that made itself felt, though neither seen nor heard, was experienced at The Place, Great Bardfield. The Place was built in the reigns of Mary and Elizabeth and the latter is said to have been given shelter here while still a Princess from the wrath of Mary. When the house was being restored in 1949 a tiny piece of parchment was found in a hole in a beam. On it was written in Latin, "O gentle Jesus, deliver us". This was probably written as a spell against plague by William Bendlowes, Sergeant-at-law in Elizabeth's reign and builder of the house. It is now the home of John Aldridge, the artist, who told me that the house is said to be haunted and, before the war, they did have some complaints from guests about being woken up in the night by an unhappy female presence. Nobody saw anything, but they woke up unexpectedly and thought something had woken them; they had the feeling there was a woman about whose distress had disturbed them. They all seemed to agree about the sensation, although no one reported hearing a voice. One friend, a level headed business woman, later confessed she had always been frightened to go into the bathroom at night. She was not aware that the bathroom, though approached by a separate passage, had originally been part of the bedroom where disquiet was felt.

About half a dozen people, more or less independently, spoke of vague discomfort they had experienced, although none gave any precise sensuous evidence. After making enquiries Mr Aldridge concluded that it might have something to do with Eleanor, wife of William Bendlowes. The Bendlowes were Roman Catholics and, owing to the favour of the Queen, Mass is supposed to have been said in Great Bardfield church later than in any other. William left instructions in his will for prayers to be said for the souls of his wife, himself, King Philip and Queen Mary, but by the time he died the practice of saying prayers for the dead was illegal and the terms of his will were not carried out. Mr Aldridge says that the present day Roman Catholics say that this would be enough to make Mrs Bendlowes a restless spirit and, taking their word for it, he had the presence exorcised. Since then there have been no complaints or manifestations and friends say that atmosphere in the spare room (which may have been the best bedroom before William Bendlowes altered the house in 1564) is now perfectly serene. A rubbing of Eleanor Bendlowes' brass is her room. There is a Bendlowes Chapel in the North Aisle of St Mary the Virgin.

A ghost at Great Wakering was easily explained. Next to the church was an old house, formerly the Vicarage. A suicide had been committed here and visitors were shown bloodstains on the floor and walls. The villagers were terrified by ghostly lights moving in the house at night and a figure flitting past the windows. However, a gentleman living opposite loaded his gun with sparrow shot and waited for the ghost. When it appeared he fired, but just too late. The next morning a white sheet and other evidence in the haunted house showed that an accomplice had assisted the 'ghost' with moving candles and strings. That ghost was well and truly laid.

At another old house that had been two cottages my mother lived for some years. Old inhabitants of Wakering said that a former occupier used to bake and sell pies there about seventy years ago. In the early hours of the morning my mother often woke up to smell the most delicious odour and there seemed to be no explanation. It did not come from the bakery, as it definitely was not the smell of new-made bread and that seemed to be the only solution to the mystery of the morning, besides it came from within the house.

According to a report in the *Psychic News* of January, 1956, a harmonium that played in the night drove a young married couple from their flat in a three storey Victorian house in Southchurch Road, Southend. Five weeks after Richard and Olive Woodley moved into the flat, Olive heard footsteps on the bare boards overhead in the empty upper part of the house. Then a loud crash outside their bedroom door some nights later woke them up. The husband went to investigate, but found nothing. This was followed a few nights later by 'ghostly organ music', as they described it, which woke them at 1 a.m. Mr Woodley said that it was like somebody playing onefinger exercises. "No tune, just aimless drawnout notes. The sounds came from the upper floor and continued for a little while."

The next morning he went upstairs to investigate and found three dust-covered harmoniums which neither he nor his wife knew were there. They could only be played by moving the foot-pedals. The following night they heard the ghostly music again and they decided to leave at once. He and a friend with a photographer went back to the flat. They heard noises and footsteps, but not the harmonium. Mr Woodley suffered from nervous trouble after this and his doctor said it was probably due to his unusual experience.

A letter published in the Winter issue, 1957, of *Newscast,* the journal of the Phenomenist Research League, tells of incidents of a supernatural origin at a house, formerly a school, near Hockley church.

> When we moved to the 'Old School House' nine months ago, anything of a supernatural nature had not occurred to me, but various little incidents (doors of the old-fashioned latch type opening although they had been securely closed; tinkling bells ringing in the hall late at night, etc.) led us to presume that it was the ghost of a child who may have attended here when it

was a school from 1804 onwards and we christened it 'Matilda' lightheartedly. I keep the hall lights off after dusk in the hope that someone or something will materialise, but I have had no results so far.

M H Murgatroyd

The Old Schools at Hadleigh are said by local people to be haunted and with reason. In 1955, when the Benfleet Art Club had their Exhibition in the schools, several people were sitting quietly one evening when they heard running footsteps coming up to the entrance, they came into the building and went towards the toilets. No one could be seen, but they saw a shadow pass. In 1956, at another of the Club's Exhibitions, members of the Club were startled by a terrific noise, a clap, which considerably shocked them. It sounded in or very near the building, but nothing could be found to account for it. Shortly afterwards it came again, then someone noticed that the lights in the toilet were going on and off. Thinking that someone was playing tricks, two members investigated, but no one was there. A gentleman who spent a night there guarding valuable miniatures on exhibit said that he would not do it again as he had a very disturbed night. One night during the 1956 Exhibition some of the members locked up and left for home, but shortly after it was queried if the gas had been turned off. To make sure all was safe they returned to the schools. One lady said she felt something or someone behind the door as they opened it - an intensely 'resentful presence' who wanted them to go.

In 1826 Barry Well, a 66-year-old inhabitant of Haverhill, Suffolk, had the cheerful idea of keeping a *Book of Dismal Happenings*. One extract is

1832. John Cook, School-master at Steeple Bumpstead

died March 24th, after he was dead and buried a boy saw his apparition, he saw him go through his gate, and the gate neither opened nor shut, he was so alarm'd that he ran home and hug'd his mother by the neck.

Ruined buildings and old houses are always thought to be fit abodes for ghosts and even new houses are sometimes troubled, but surely a caravan must be free from these visitors! Mr A Morrish of Chelmsford wrote to the *Essex Chronicle* on 28th January, 1955, as follows

Gazing upward to the ceiling one night (or rather what would have been a ceiling had I been living in a house) I was meditating on nothing in particular, when I discerned the outline of a figure becoming as it were more realistic. It appeared to be that of an average sized man surrounded in pallid light. The lower portion seemed to wear large knee-length boots. Upwards I could make out what might have been apparel such as worn in Cromwell's time.

I was not alarmed, my curiosity alone was sufficient to dispel the existence of my visitant, for turning the first time to obtain a more distinct view, the phantom, if such he was, receded into darkness.

Imagination or an ostracised ghost? I don't know, But so vivid was my experience that night in a caravan in rural Essex that I recorded the occurrence on the following morning.

A 17th century record, the examination of a servant who stole some geese at Basildon, tells how she saw a ghost. In 1650 Susan Lay, three days after the burial of her mistress, saw her ghost appear all in white one night as she lay in a barn in Battlesbridge. Three nights it appeared and on the third night it called her name and pinched her on its departure! It appeared again in the barn on a Sunday night when it was seen by several other people. The next day Susan, with another girl, walked to Basildon and near 'Basseldon' Hall she took a couple of geese and killed them while her companion kept watch. They carried the geese to Billericay and tried to sell them, afterwards taking them to Hutton and eating them.

At North Benfleet is a wood adjoining the land of Fanton Hall, which was known as Shrieking Boy, or Screeching Boy's, Wood. It was said to be so called because here a ploughman killed his plough-boy with his plough spud. According to the church registers a murder was committed on Fanton Hall Farm in 1734 and this seems to support the legend. A more colourful version is that, in a fit of temper, a woodsman working in the copse at the end of Kingsley Lane cut off his working boy's head because he was not working hard enough. Hiding the torso in a hollow tree the woodsman told the local people who asked about the boy that he had run away. The woodsman, so the story goes, was haunted by the boy he had murdered and used to get drunk in the Hart at Thundersley to try and stop the bloodcurdling screams coursing through his head. The boy was supposed to sit on the gate at the entrance to the wood now and then and scream when anyone approached, to remind them of his murder. Some children a few years ago went to see if the legend was true. Sure enough, sitting on the gate was a screaming figure: they fled without ascertaining if it was a headless ghost.

Grays has a haunted fire station. It was reported some years ago that a former fire chief was unable to leave Grays Fire Station, although he had been dead twenty years. Divisional Officer Johnny Jones made late night appearances in the dormitory, appearing as a shadow dressed in officer's uniform. He was often seen, but never regularly - some of the firemen who saw the ghost did not know the history of the station, yet their descriptions of the apparition are identical to those seen before.

One afternoon in October, 1984, Mr K O Jones woke from a doze he had been enjoying in an armchair in a 1897 house, 38 Parkstone Avenue, Emerson Park, Hornchurch, to see a little girl in Edwardian costume, who said, "Can I have my ball back, please?" He rubbed his eyes and she had gone. What Mr Jones did not know was that his son-in-law had found a painted rubber ball under the floorboards in an upstairs room three days earlier.

Told by Rev Rowland Jones in *Prediction* January, 1952.

Borley Church

More ghosts of cottage, farm and mansion

Goldsmiths Manor, standing on the southern slopes of Langdon Hills, was the country seat of Sir Joseph Dimsdale, Lord Mayor of London in 1901-2. The original house was built in the 18th century, but on either side are modern additions by Sir Joseph. In three of the ancient attics, once the sleeping place of the maidservants, strange tappings are heard and ghostly footsteps have also been heard on the stairs at night. One lady who slept in the attic at the head of the stairs heard these noises and felt such a horrible atmosphere that she had to get up in the night and put her head out of the window. A guest asked if her host had to go out one night as she heard footsteps on the stairs, but no one had been on the stairs that night.

One misty night the lady of the house was on her own as her husband was in Paris and it was too foggy for him to fly home. On coming into the hall in the old part of the building from the kitchen with a cup of tea on a tray she noticed a lady standing to one side of the hall. She wondered vaguely how she had got there and noticed that she wore no outdoor clothes, although it was such an inclement night. As she was going to ask what she wanted the woman vanished before her eyes. Feeling very shocked she managed to walk into the sitting room and put the tray down, but her pet pug dog began to howl and kept on howling.

That evening she went to a friend's house and they commented that she 'looked as if she had seen a ghost'.

"As a matter of fact, I have," she replied and told them

of her experience. On describing the ghostly lady's appearance and clothes - she wore a beige tucked dress - her friend's husband said the description fitted a former inhabitant of Goldsmiths.

Not far from Goldsmiths stood, until 1933 when it was destroyed by fire, the ancient timber farmhouse of Northlands, which was probably 300 years old. Its kitchen had a most uncanny atmosphere and a door in it would always open by some invisible agency. Blood stains on the floorboards in another part of the house were said to come from a man who had committed suicide.

Elizabethan Marks Hall, near Kelvedon, demolished in 1951, was haunted by Cromwell's soldiers who dug the lakes near the house. During the siege of Colchester Cromwell is said to have made his head quarters at the Hall. The lady who was the last resident of the house often saw the ghosts of the soldiers, who she thought were friendly fellows, and said that on several occasions she was hailed by them in her bedroom. Often she said, "Hello, soldier."

She recalled, "Marks Hall was to me the most peaceful and friendly house, but I was not the only one who met these friendly Puritan soldiers. A cook-housekeeper never saw the house before she came to live there, but asked for another room after her first night in the house. She said she was 'in a fair sweat'. A gentleman came into the room, with hat plumes, cape and sword. She screamed and switched on the light: he faded out. Her room was in the Jacobean wing.

"In 1941 a hundred men were billeted in the house. The colonel paid me a visit, as C.O.s always did. He said, 'I have an officer ill in a room. He says he will not stay another night in that room. The door opens softly and closes, off and or, and there is a rustle.' I laughed and said, 'It is one of Cromwell's soldiers come to see what yours are like!'

This was also in the Jacobean wing. There was nothing evil in the house. I loved it and was so happy there. In one of the beautifully panelled rooms on the ground floor Cromwell held a daily service for his troops, prayers and psalms, his extempore prayers were very fine, and that room was called the Prayer Room and Room of Humiliation."

The Hall was exactly as it was when Cromwell was there, except for the 60 feet dining room added in 1702. Singing had been heard in that room.

Another historic mansion suffering the same fate as Marks Hall was Belhus, Aveley, demolished in 1956. A former servant there had memories both of the ghost and of the conditions in the house at the end of last century. As there were no bathrooms hot water had to be carried by the maids to the bedrooms. Brass cans hung on the walls of the servants' quarters and the maids filled them, carrying two at a time upstairs. One evening the lady says she was carrying her cans up the front staircase to the dressing rooms; lighted candles were set on the banister post and she passed the naked plaster lady on the first corner, then the man on the second corner, when suddenly in the light of the flickering candles she saw an elderly figure in black silk and lace rustle past her. She dropped the cans where she stood and ran to Sir Thomas Barrett Lennard's room, where he was dressing for dinner. "Where, where, show me where," he said, and rushed with her to where she had left the cans. He told her to go downstairs and make sure the front door was locked, then they searched the whole building, but could find nothing. Everyone was scared and after that they never went around alone after dark. Her mother used to go round the house between four and five o'clock at night and one evening in the Tapestry Room she felt cold hands on her shoulders. The former maid always believed the ghost lived behind a locked door in the hall downstairs and she was never told what was behind it or found the key. When the mansion was pulled down she intended to go over the house to see, but although arrangements were made at the last minute she was unable to go.

Was there any connection between the ghosts of Belhus and rats? For the worst trouble was rats as big as cats and very tame. Sir Thomas would not let them be killed, so everything had to be kept under covers. The noise they made was like people running up and down the corridors, which may account for the footsteps heard on the flagstones leading from the kitchen. Another story of Belhus is that the form of a female domestic was sometimes seen haunting the galleries and stairs between the rooms. She was seen on one occasion in an armchair in a bedroom. Fred Claro said that Belhus Mansion had a private chapel, authentic ghost, secret chamber and the tradition of a visit by Queen Elizabeth I. He stated that two of the daughters of the steward who lived in the mansion experienced several mysterious happenings that could not be accounted for. At night on several occasions when they were fast asleep they would be woken by a presence in the bedroom. Those who caught a glimpse of the ghost said it was a shadowy figure in a black cloak.

The home of the maid who had the frightening experience on the stairs at Belhus was also haunted, by old Tom, who was supposed to have committed suicide in, of all places, the outside earth closet!

Little Sampford Hall, demolished many years ago, was held by the wealthy and notable Grene family, devout Catholics who paid many fines for their faith. Three members of the family were buried at midnight and it may be assumed that these funerals were attended by a priest hidden in the house. A Lady Grene is reputed to have killed herself in one of the attics or bathrooms and her restless spirit afterwards haunted the old house. Although one, Sir Edward Grene, gambled away the large estate and house the ghost still disturbed the peace of the mansion.

While in the hands of its last owner the house was haunted at various periods. Lights were seen in windows and bedroom doorknobs turned and it was thought that the mysterious lights along the corridors coincided with the dates of the secret midnight burials of the Grene family [*Essex Countryside* January, 1969]. An aged lady once a maid at the hall during the time it was inhabited by its last owner told of seeing lights flitting from window to window and, especially memorable, was one terrifying night when she and the other maids listened in dread to the knob of her bedroom door being constantly turned by the ghost of Lady Grene. When the mansion was demolished its early 17th century staircase was sent to the United States. What happened to the ghost? Did she go to America or does she still haunt the site on which another house now stands?

At Stondon Massey there is or was the 18th century Jordan ghost. It is said with some uncertainty to be that of Richard Jordan, who built Stondon Place, destroyed by fire in 1866. At his burial no less than eleven clergymen assisted. Afterwards the sexton on several occasions peering into the vault to see if all was well found the corpse lying outside the coffin. Eventually the remains were chained down. A more prosaic explanation is that, at the time, it was not uncommon to secure a coffin with chains to stop bodysnatching. After this, the ghost appeared and all sorts of tales circulated about it. The ghost was seen hovering about the churchyard late at night terrifying passers by. One man returning from Ongar with a scythe met the ghost and tried to mow it down; as he tried to decapitate the figure his own arm remained poised in the air paralysed and helpless. Reports were current that in the deceased gentleman's lifetime he was overheard conversing with the Evil One and that he wrote by the Devil's aid in fiery characters on the walls of his home. If this particular Jordan was a retired medical man (one or more of his descendants were) he may have played a practical joke on his credulous fellow-parishioners.

The most inexplicable incident attributed to the Jordan ghost happened in 1841 when the rector of Bobbingworth and his wife were asked to dine with Mr P H Meyer at Stondon Place. They started from home in a closed carriage drawn by two horses, the postboy riding one of them. At Shelley House they took up Captain Kirsterman and his wife and the two gentlemen rode on the box seat, while the wives sat inside. It was a fine bright evening and all went well until they arrived at the front gate of Stondon Place, when nothing would induce the horses to pass through it. The post-boy whipped and spurred and the gentlemen urged, all to no effect. The ladies, very frightened, alighted and walked to the house. During the evening fellow guests were most interested in this thrilling event. When they departed everyone turned out to see them start. The carriage, which had been taken to the stables by another gate, was brought to the front door and the Olivers and Kirstermans took their places. The journey was smooth enough to the gate, when again the horses stopped, snorted and absolutely refused to pass through. After the host had offered the two couples hospitality for the night and Mr Oliver had said it was necessary to return, Mr Meyer ordered out his own carriage to convey them home. All this was attributed to the Jordan Ghost, then said to be freely walking in Stondon. About 1845 it was said to be seen gliding silently by the Rectory to disappear among the trees near the National School.

A more humble ghost is that of a farmer's daughter who, hundreds of years ago, at Upper Wyburn's Farm, Dawes Heath, Thundersley, drowned herself in the farm pond because her father would not let her get married. About 1917 five people saw the ghostly figure dripping wet on the second stile leading to the London Road from Dawes Heath Road. The band of youngsters was returning across the fields from Leigh at 9 o'clock at night when reaching the stile they saw a grey shape. On a close look it appeared to be the dripping figure of a female form with a stony expressionless face just staring at them without a single movement. All five turned and fled.

According to a report in the *Southend Standard* of 30 May, 1963, there have been strange happenings at Canewdon Vicarage. The wife of a past vicar several times saw a ghost of a young girl standing in the driveway. There is a similarity between this ghost and that of Wyburn's Farm, for she is supposed to be the daughter of a vicar and, as she fell in love with a farm worker, she was not allowed to marry him and was later found dead. The man who found her shook all over and could not stop shaking for the rest of his life. The vicar, Rev N J Kelly, who refuses to believe tales of the supernatural in the village, is reported to have said that on many occasions the doors in his house have swung open on their own, even when he had just shut them. He insisted that this was because of earth subsidence. "Is this explanation right?" the report ended.

In the *Local Review* of 8 February, 1961, there was a report of a little old lady of Hadleigh, who once owned the 400-year-old grocery shop, the Village Stores in the High Street, coming back fifty years after her death. It happened just after midnight one August night in 1960, when the then owner, Mrs I Sanderson, was in her living room ironing.

She was alone as her husband was working. A door opened from the shop into the living room and at the other end of the same wall was another door secured by a latch, which led to the two upstairs rooms. The door from the shop suddenly swung open. Mrs Sanderson stared at the open door; then turning, she saw the latched door was open. The time in between was just enough for some one to have walked from one door to the other, but Mrs Sanderson was alone in the room and the evening outside was calm. Cold with fear, Mrs Sanderson dashed upstairs and dived into bed fully clothed and lay with her head under the blankets. She lay awake all night. "When the doors opened I did not feel anything - like a rush of cold wind or anything. I did feel scared though and just ran," said Mrs Sanderson. The next evening the doors opened again. Once more the weather was calm. This time, however, Mrs Sanderson did not run; during the day she had been told something about the little old lady of Hadleigh. It was over 50 years ago that the little lady owned the stores. She was well known because she was said to fall asleep when serving customers. She loved her shop spending all her time in it until she died.

The next owner of the shop was said to have seen the old lady after her death. Since then other people have told how they saw her walk at night from the parish churchyard across the High Street and into her shop. But this is the first known time the little old lady of Hadleigh has visited her old shop before March. The night after her second visit Mrs Sanderson and her sister, Maud, sat up until the early hours waiting for another visit but the little lady did not call back.

The Moat Farm at Clavering, scene of the famous Moat Farm Murder, had a heavy studded door on the landing which was never locked, as old legend said it would open of its own accord if ever it was closed.

Poltergeists haunt two old houses in Harwich, one said to have been used as a bakery by Nelson. A bedroom door was opened by an invisible hand, crockery and glass broke of their own accord and once a glass bowl of shrimps burst into fragments.

A ghost caused an overtime ban and delayed a £100,000 contract in 1980. The work on 300-years-old Woolston Hall, now a country club, at Chigwell was due to be completed on 5th July, but at the end of June workmen fled in fear as the ghost shuffled along the third floor. The carpenter, Peter Smith, said there was no way they would work in that place at night. He became aware of an unusual presence when he was working alone on the third floor. "Suddenly the temperature dropped and I heard a weird shuffling sound. Then I heard knocking and the sound of breaking glass. I packed up and got out pretty quick."

Terry Payne said, "I don't scare easily, but this was really spooky. I was shivering and could feel the hair on my neck standing up."

It happened to several men working alone at night and all of them refused to go near the third floor after dark. The story is that a 13-year-old girl, Agnes, leapt to her death from a third-floor window at the Hall more than two centuries ago and that it is she who is the restless spirit, perhaps the alterations upset her. A director of the Epping Forest Country Club called in a psychic researcher in a bid to lay the ghost who only seemed to haunt men.

A more humble dwelling, 17th century Hill Farm, Vange, had a less vigorous ghost. W C Cartwright told me that in 1930 his godmother, Mrs Pryse, lived there. He recalls a passage led to the pantry and she said she heard voices when she was there and that the place was haunted.

Did the resident ghost move with a cottage when it was

taken from Rayleigh to Pitsea? 300-year-old Holly Cottage was dismantled and rebuilt in Wat Tyler Park. Miss Ida Laurence, who once lived in the cottage, remembers many strange goings on. Mats put on the table went back into the drawer on their own and fruit in a dish was removed and placed somewhere else. At times there was a strange feeling of something being in the cottage. Miss Laurence, however, was not frightened; she did not think it was an evil spirit, but friendly. Its true identity is a mystery: some say it is a young Victorian girl. After the dismantling of the cottage and all that entailed it seems hardly likely that it came along with the timbers. Maybe it roams disconsolately on the site of its old home - only time will tell.

About a hundred and fifty years ago a family named Wheel from Dawes Heath moved into a thatched cottage, built about 1700 or earlier, in Church Road, Thundersley. It was a tied cottage to Jarvis Hall and then had irregular ceilings, uneven floors and no drainage. The Wheels had a large family and two of the sons died in the Crimea. Old Mrs Wheel always said they tried to reach her from the spirit world by blowing a trumpet at the dead of night. She was a white witch, a renowned church-goer and lived to be a hundred years old. Wheel Cottage is now a charming dwelling with a tiled roof and the sequel is that about twenty-four years ago the Latchford family moved into the cottage and soon after Mrs Latchford used to be woken up by the sound of bugles. One night she looked at her watch and saw it was 3.15 and subsequently she worked out that each time she heard the bugles it was the time of the new moon. Her family at first laughed at her, but she so convinced them that her husband agreed that he too heard the bugles in spite of the fact that he was deaf in one ear. Her son tried to tape the sound, but was not successful. Over the early part of their life in the cottage she heard the bugles many times and now she is really quite disappointed that she has not had that pleasure for many years. At no time could this have been auto-suggestion, as she knew nothing of the history of the two bugler sons of Mrs Wheel.

For five years a woman living in a council house in Cromwell Road, Grays, was dogged by bad luck that she attributed to the phantom of a child of about four years old, a thin, frail infant with fair hair. On the first occasion she was seen a death in the family followed soon after the second time was a few days before an accident to one of the family. It was believed that the girl died there from polio during World War II.

A family in Abbotts Drive, Stanford-le-Hope, had to call in the rector to lay the ghost that was terrorizing them. The ghost tapped on windows and moved small objects around the house He was seen standing on the doorstep and near a dustbin in the front garden. Footsteps were heard coming downstairs and then the front room door where they were sitting - opened and closed. They also felt they were watched and the family of five felt cold breath on their necks. Knives, scissors and a hammer have gone missing and beef cubes in the kitchen cupboard were missing when wanted. A week later the cubes were back in the cupboard in the place where they had originally been placed. The dogs sensed that there was something and their hair stood on end. The wife thought the haunting could be connected with Abbotts Hall, the farm once owned by Waltham Abbey, as the house is built on the farm site. Another opinion is that the ghost may have been brought to the house by a member of the family.

Lastly, Spaynes Hall, Great Yeldham, has a ghost, a certain Richard Hughes; who he was is not known and he has not been seen recently.

Ghosts of castles and religious houses

The oldest ghost connected with a former Essex religious building is St Osyth, over a thousand years old, who is said to roam the grounds of St Osyth Priory one night a year. Osyth was the daughter of Frithwald, the first Christian King of the East Angles. Although she would rather have been a nun, her parents betrothed her to Sighere, King of Essex. At the marriage feast news was brought of a fine white stag; Sighere at once set out in pursuit. Osyth took advantage of this remarkable opportunity and fled to a nunnery, where she took the veil. Sighere on his return realised that nothing could be done about the marriage, so he very generously gave Osyth the village of Chich, where she founded a nunnery.

Osyth was happy as the Abbess of her nunnery until one day in 653 when Danish pirates sailed up the creek. They sacked the convent and, when Osyth refused to worship their gods, they struck off her head. Osyth at once rose and picked up her head and walked to the church, where she knocked on the door with one of her bloodstained hands and then fell dead. Where her head fell a stream of water gushed forth and the stream in Nun's Wood still runs. Here, one night a year, St Osyth comes bearing her head in her hands.

Cherry Lane, near the ruins of Tilty Abbey, was said to be haunted by a headless monk. One day the Vicar made some excavations on the site; under a 13th century stone coffin lid, a skeleton was found complete except for the skull. The explanation may well be that when the Abbot resisted the pillaging of the Abbey by King John's army in 1215, one of the brethren was decapitated. For 700 years a memory of this deed has lingered on in the belief of the phantom of the headless monk.

Little remains of the Abbey, apart from the parish church, which was once part of the complex, there are only a few pieces of low wall in a meadow; these are said to be part of the cloisters. It is supposed to be most unlucky to remove any materials from the Abbey, but nevertheless Tilty folk and others have not let this deter them from taking the stones, as the small fragment remaining proves. About 130 years ago several buildings remained that were used as farm buildings. The tradition was that if anyone ordered any of these buildings to be demolished he would die within a month. A steward did so - and did so! His successor of the same family ordered some more buildings to be pulled down and he, too, died within a month. There is the usual story that an underground passage leads from the Abbey - this time to Horham Hall, three miles away.

The precincts of Waltham Abbey are reputed to be haunted; soldiers on guard in 1944 were scared by an invisible presence that tugged at their coats and performed similar disconcerting acts. So scared were the soldiers that they refused to go on guard alone.

Many of the legends connected with monastic houses, especially if they are ruins, came from the superstitious awe felt by the villagers when the monks were driven out and the holy buildings desecrated. They naturally felt it would be unlucky to touch materials from the church and that the spirits of the monks would haunt the place they loved and were driven from.

When I visited Latton Priory, now a farm, the farmer's wife said that there were no ghosts, but the doors of the barn (which was once part of the priory church) are said to open every night at midnight. When first she came to the farm someone told her that a man on a white horse rode round the moat every night, but she suspected leg pulling! The fine columns of the church, remains of the nave and crossing and parts of the north and south transepts are disfigured with names cut in the stone. Instead of the monk's chant a robin sang his sad little autumn song. I reflected that the priors and monks would be buried nearby. Between the farmhouse and the barn was the cloister-garth and here, when a hole was dug for a post, the coffin of a canon was found. For 400 years farmers have stored their corn and threshed it here, until the only reminder of the ancient priory of the Black Canons is the lovely stone columns. The bodies of the monastic brethren have passed into dust - gone and forgotten, as are the labourers whose hands helped raise the priory church.

When visiting Beeleigh Abbey I enquired if the ghosts of the monks ever walked the place and received the reply, "The only ghosts are the ones you see here!" and a little door was opened at the end of the dorter where two people were about to enter, at least that is what we first thought, then we discovered we were looking at the reflections of ourselves in a mirror facing the door in a small passage leading to landing and stairs. There is, however, a ghost. One of the Abbots haunts the James Room and a previous owner saw him on one occasion. This room contains a beautiful carved wooden bed on which James I slept, although not in this house. The ghost is said to walk the oak-beamed bedroom once a year on 13th April.

At Pleshey only the earthworks and a single-span bridge of 15th century date remain to remind us of the castle from whence Richard II lured his Uncle, the Duke of Gloucester, to his death, but in connection with that dark deed there is a legend still told in the village that his duchess lived there for some time after that, but her gold and silver were put into a big chest and cast into the moat. Others, however, say that a big chest reputed to contain treasure was sunk into the moat on the destruction of Pleshey College of priests. Anyway, a big, iron-bound chest is said to lie in the 'black moat' or outer moat that no one has been able to drag up. Once it is said to have been pulled out by a strong train of horses, but the rope broke and it slid back into the water.

There is also a ghost. A lady sitting in the kitchen of Pleshey Mount Farm at twilight one winter evening saw a nun pass the window. This seemed rather unusual, so she went to the door to see what the nun wanted, but, on looking out, there was no sign of her; there was nothing to hide her and, moreover, there had not been time for her to walk far, she had simply vanished. When her brother came in she told him of the vanishing nun and he said, "You have seen the ghost; I have often seen it." Isabel, a daughter of the murdered Duke of Gloucester, became a nun: could it have been her apparition that was seen?

Prittlewell Priory has a ghost story, but it is not about the monks as might be imagined. A former owner of post-monastic times cut his throat so badly that his head was said to be nearly severed. Ever since the Priory has been reputed to be haunted by his ghost. Some folk believed implicitly in this apparition. The local press once reported that a number of monks had been seen mysteriously filing into Prittlewell church at dusk, but that no one had seen any monks come out! Were they ghosts of the ancient inhabitants of the Priory, it was asked. No, the rather disappointing and very matter-of-fact explanation was that the monks were local people dressed for a rehearsal for a procession to be held in the town. They entered the church at the Rector's invitation and changed their clothes before leaving one by one. However, ghostly monks have been seen at the Priory. One of the attendants at the Priory Museum told me that he saw a monk standing in the doorway of the refectory that leads to the entrance hall. It was daylight and it only appeared for a second or so. The same man was talking to a young policewoman in the cloister garth when he saw something on the ground, but he did not take much notice, then it appeared to be a body rising towards him, then it vanished. The policewoman did not see anything. There is also a report that a medium visiting the Priory once saw several monks walking on the lawns where the priory church once stood. The squawking of ducks on the priory pond is said to warn of the Ghostly Monk: a doubtful story.

I have not heard that there were ever any ghostly visitors at Thoby Priory, but skeletons were found walled up in part of the Priory buildings and a curious discovery was made when alterations were being carried out at the beginning of the last century. Bacon, black with age and smoke, was found hanging in the chimney. It was supposed that it had remained there from the days before the dissolution of the monastery, but even stranger was the fact that the workmen ate the bacon and pronounced it excellent! The house at Thoby Priory was demolished some years ago and only a few ruins of the church remain.

Hadleigh Castle has several ghostly tales told about it. A woman in white was once said to haunt the ruins. A milkmaid from the Castle Farm saw her early one morning and was commanded to meet her at the Castle at midnight, when she would disclose mysteries connected with the ruins. However, the girl was too frightened to obey the command. The next morning the white lady met her unexpectedly and was very annoyed that she had not appeared the previous night and she cuffed the girl so hard over the ear that her neck was almost dislocated. There after the girl was known as 'Wry-neck Sal'. Whether this story is to do with the fact that the Castle ruins were used by a gang of smugglers, of whom Dick Turpin was one, in the 18th century cannot be said, but the gang used to burn coloured lights that frightened the superstitious inhabitants who believed the ruins to be haunted by evil spirits.

Colne Priory at Earls Colne was founded by Aubrey de Vere for black monks of the Order of St Benedict It was so close to the river that tradition says the monks used to fish out of the windows. Only part of the northwest tower of the church remains above ground at the present day; an 18th century house has taken its place. By the late 17th century the remains of the choir of the priory church had been divided into two, one part serving as a sleeping apartment for servants, while the other, known as the monument house, contained 'olde monuments with other lumber'. It was said to be haunted.

Servants sleeping there said that every night at two o'clock they were awakened and alarmed by the boom of a great bell. Colonel Richard Harlackenden, a staunch Puritan and senior officer of Oliver Cromwell, was annoyed by their statements and ordered a bed to be made up for him in the chamber. In the middle of the night, when he was in a deep sleep, he was woken at the stated time by the stroke of a bell. No longer sceptical, he hastily left his bed and ran out of the room.

Coggeshall Abbey, on the banks of the Blackwater, has an even older ghost story. About the period 1176-94 some 'ghostly templars' were found one day in the guest house by Robert, the assistant hosteller. Thinking they were men of great importance he went at once to arrange that they should dine with the Abbot in his private quarters. On his return they had vanished. The Chronicle states 'who these men were, how they came or whether they departed, remains unknown even to this day'.

Hadleigh Castle as seen by John Constable

Ghosts of royalty and nobility

Probably the most famous individual to haunt any Essex house is Anne Boleyn, who is reputed to appear in at least two places in the county. At New Hall, Boreham, once the residence of Henry Vlll, her ghost is said to haunt the grounds, but she has not been seen in recent years. It is not surprising if she does roam the precincts of New Hall, as here she spent many happy days with her royal lover.

Rochford Hall is another place where Anne appears at midnight, but there is no more reliable evidence than the tales told by an old lady who was caretaker there many years ago. She used to show a stain in the floor of a room in the tower where she said Anne was beheaded! She also told an old Rochford inhabitant that one day she saw a pretty lady dressed in quaint clothes standing at the foot of the stairs. She asked her whom she wanted to see and, at that, the lady just faded away. Anne, she said, was often seen about the place. If she hoped to make an impression on visitors so that they would suitably reward her, she failed dismally, for no one ever believed her, which is hardly surprising after her statement about the tower room. However, unexplainable footsteps have been heard by a family who lived in the hall for many years. A son of the family used to sometimes return home after the others were in bed and at first the footsteps were thought to be his until it was found that on several occasions they could not have been, as he had not been out or was already in bed by that time. They always referred to these footsteps as being those of Anne, never thinking of it being anyone else.

When a tall slim wooden cross was removed from the summit of the tower of Boleyn Castle, West Ham, before it was demolished, it was said that Anne's ghost would appear, but it did not. Boleyn Castle is said to have been a hunting lodge of Henry's, who is reputed to have built the tower for Anne to see the shipping on the river and, that when his jealousy was first aroused at the tournament at Greenwich, he shut her up in this tower, before moving her to the Tower of London.

Although Queen Elizabeth I visited Essex quite a lot on her progresses, the only place she haunts is Horham Hall, Thaxted. It is related in the *Essex Review* of July, 1896, that many years previously a groom at Horham Hall had fallen into bad ways and was in the habit of arriving home at very late hours. One night, as he crept up to his room, he was terrified to hear the distinct tap-tap of the royal lady's high heeled shoes coming after him. He rushed into his room and, covering his head with the bedclothes, vowed he would never be late again. He kept his word too! Her Majesty must, however, have deserted the Hall, as Sir George Binney said he never had any psychic experience nor has anyone else, so far as he was aware.

It is noted in the *Essex Review* of January, 1930, that Cilwell Hall in the hamlet of Sewardstone on the Essex border had a ghost that used to walk along the corridor and open a bedroom door. It was reputed to be that of a frequent visitor to Gilwell, Adolphus Frederick, first Duke of Cambridge and seventh son of George III.

At Otes Pond, High Laver, stood the house where Abigail Masham, the friend and confidant of Queen Anne, came to live after the Queen's death. Through the influence of Sarah Churchill, first Duchess of Marlborough, Abigail was appointed Woman of the Bedchamber to Anne. She was really a kind of dresser to the Queen, handing her garments to the Lady of the Bedchamber who put them on the Queen and doing all sorts of small personal things for her. Abigail's sweet and gentle nature endeared her to Anne and, after the Queen had quarrelled with the Duchess of Marlborough, Abigail became an important power with the Queen. In 1707 Abigail was married privately at night to Samuel Masham of High Laver and in 1711 was created Keeper of the Privy Purse and her husband became a Baron. Abigail worked for the Tory cause and became a leader of the Jacobite party, but on the Queen's death she retired to High Laver. Although her house was demolished in the last century, it is still said that on Christmas Eve a phantom carriage drives through the village and draws up where the house formerly stood and a lady, presumably Abigail, looks sadly about her before she and her carriage fade away. Most people dismiss it as nonsense today, but some have sat up through the night to watch for it, but have been disappointed.

At Great Easton the wind now sighs over the site of Easton Lodge. There is a well-authenticated story of how, when it was standing, the ghost of the Countess of Warwick, once the toast of the fashionable and great, walked down the grand staircase at dead of night. Soldiers billeted there during World War II were scared when they returned to their quarters one night and saw a shrouded figure slowly descending this staircase. They took to their heels, but from their description of the figure it was doubtless the ghost of the Countess they had seen.

Ghosts of the roads and lanes

It must have been nerve-wracking to make some journeys in Essex at night in a more superstitious age, for many roads are haunted - or so reputed. Like other counties there are tales of phantom coaches and headless horses.

Many years ago a farmer and his wife living in the neighbourhood of Clavering were returning home from Saffron Walden market; the old chap, half dozing, set the horses at a steady pace, when suddenly there was a jingle of harness and the sound of approaching galloping hooves. The farmer, thinking it was another waggon, hastily pulled over to the grass verge. The noise grew louder, then died away. The old people were convinced that a phantom coach had passed them that night on the lonely road.

Is it possible to see ghosts and not know they are ghosts? Mrs Cranwell of Chrishall did and it was not until twenty years later that she realised that she, her father and her brother had at Clavering years before. The story, as she wrote it, is

About 1932/3 on a Friday night when the lilacs were in bloom I was cycling home from choir practise and had to negotiate a little watercourse, known as The King's Water, that crossed the road. A three-plank wide bridge crossed the stream. It was a favourite spot for courting couples and from the bridge a path led at right-angles across the fields. It was in the dimpsey light, not really dark although the sun had set, there was a glow in the sky. As I rode my bicycle down the hill I noticed that two people were on the bridge: they looked oddly familiar. The boy sat on the top rail of the bridge with his left arm around the girl's shoulders. As I drew nearer I thought, "Oh, bother, Tichy and Ethel are on the bridge." They often met there. "Now I shall have to ride through the water." But I was struck how pretty Ethel looked. She had on a cream coloured dress of some soft material and it was patterned all over with little pink roses in groups of three and she had a filmy white fichu thing around her shoulders. The dress seemed a bit long and had a deep frill or flounce around the bottom - I can see it in my mind's eye now. Very, very pretty. By the time I had got to the bridge they had moved away and I assumed they had sauntered along the field path and I was able to ride over the bridge and when I got along the road it struck me I had not seen them open or climb over a gate into the fields; glancing over my shoulder I saw that the couple were once more back on the bridge. Beyond a 'warm peace', a lovely sensation, whenever I crossed the bridge afterwards I thought no more of it. Over twenty years later my father died and some weeks after my brother and I were talking and he told me a most unusual tale. My brother had a lovely singing voice and between the wars was engaged at times to sing at special events - the journeys were always by bicycle. When he came home one night he looked into my father's bedroom for the usual little chat after an evening out. He said, "We talked for a little while and then I said to him, 'Tichy and Ethel are out late tonight. They are still at King's Water Bridge.' Dad looked at me a bit oddly I thought, then he said, 'That isn't Tichy and Ethel, boy - they've been there for years.' I said, 'What do you mean? Are they ghosts? Have you seen them ?' And Dad said, 'Cor, think I have, boy, hundreds of times, but they'll never hurt you."' As my brother finished the anecdote it suddenly dawned on me that that was what I had seen all those years before and I said, "Hey, I've seen them too," and told him how pretty 'Ethel' had looked in her rose dotted cream dress. Manlike, he said, "I can only remember she had a sort of white lady thing round her shoulders" - the fichu that took my eye, no doubt. Now, had I heard anything of the story before I might subconsciously have imagined that I saw the couple, but for nearly a quarter of a century I had no idea that the story existed and that the bridge was haunted. I did see them. They were lovely, certainly not frightening, quite the reverse.

Mrs Cranwell does not know what their story was, but thought it must have been a beautiful one to leave such a feeling of serenity, an aura of peace. "I feel it still when I go that was," she wrote, "Alas a road bridge has been made over the stream, but I hope they still meet there."

There was a tradition that suicides were buried at different times at the cross-roads immediately to the south of Prislings, Dagenham, and this may be connected with the belief current years ago with the old inhabitants of Dagenham that ghosts and other phenomena had been seen at this spot. A coach drawn by four headless horses was seen at midnight on at least two occasions to the great terror of the witnesses [Shawcross: *History of Dagenham,* 1908]. The area is now built up and there is no marked recollection of the headless horses.

Sir Harbottle Grimston may still be seen noiselessly travelling through Bradfield village on still, moonlight nights in his coach and four. Sir Harbottle resided at Bradfield Hall in Stuart days, being a member of the Parliament that impeached Archbishop Laud, later becoming Speaker of the House of Commons.

A lady told me that, as a child, she used to hear the older folk talk about a lady who rode a white horse haunting Sandy Hills, between Wormingford and Bures. Perhaps there was some confusion with the apparition of the horseman 'who shone in the dark' and haunted the road from Bures to Lamarsh Hill by night, terrifying all he met. The parson went alone to deal with him, but he could not read the exorcism fast enough and the ghost was so strong that it jumped on his back and knocked him over. The end of it all was that the parsons of Bures St Mary, Mount Bures and Wormingford, with their clerks, wardens and choirs, went to the spot bringing a candle which they lit. They then read the ghost down into it and, according to the legend, told him that he was not to come out until the candle had burnt out, but, while the candle was still alight, they put it under the stub of an elder. The elder stub was burnt shortly afterwards and that was the end of 'Old Crisp', as the ghost was generally known. This may have taken place about 1800-30 [Dr T Wood: *True Thomas*].

Mr J H Newman of Bridge Street, Bures, told the author that "There has always been a tale of a headless woman, carrying her head under her arm, who appeared at the bridge over Craig's Brook at Mount Bures at midnight. This is a lonely spot at the foot of two steep hills and I know that people were afraid to go there at night time."

Miss E Vaughan, in the *Essex Review* of April, 1941,

told of ghostly footsteps that could be heard at twilight in the deeply cut lane that led downhill to a wayside brook at Rayne. She had heard the mysterious steps of the unseen wayfarers herself. However, the road is now straight, broad and curbed and the footsteps are no longer heard.

Dick Turpin made such an impression that he is supposed to haunt a number of places. One of these is Stock Road, Billericay, between the Hospital and Hill House Drive approximately. Many years ago a resident of Stock, making his way homewards, met a horseman in this part and spoke to him. As he received no answer of any kind he knew it was a ghost, his daughter said, which hardly seems proof; the rider might have been deaf. This part of Stock Road formerly had ponds and overhanging trees and its scenery doubtless helped to make it haunted by repute, if not in fact.

Dick also gallops down Trap's Hill, Loughton, three times each year. An old woman, said to be the ghost of a woman he once tortured by fire to reveal her hidden gold, jumps up behind him at one point on the journey and anyone who sees them has lasting misfortune.

In March, 1951, the people of Bardfield were scared as they walked home by night by a grey shape that came out from behind trees and from shadows. Those who saw it claimed it was the ghost of a man and that they would not go along the street after dark any more.

Molram's Lane, Great Baddow, is haunted by the ghost of Maria or Mollie Ram, who owned land in Baddow in the 16th century. She is one of the many legendary ghosts that are said to walk at certain spots, although nobody living has seen them they are probably founded on fact and are folk memories.

Mrs M Blake of Wickham Bishops wrote me the following

Until a few years ago there grew by the end of 'Bringey' footpath, Great Baddow, at the junction of Molram's Lane and Sandon Road, a thicket of gorse bushes and 'twas here, so I was told, that once lived an old woman called Mol Ram. I Imagine her, an ancient crone, bent over a fire or sticks before her ramshackle, furze-thatched hut. She was a wise woman with healing powers and many sought her aid.

Others there were who feared her and called her a witch and one night, after some calamity had befallen the village, an angry mob from Sandon fell upon Moll Ram with sticks and stones and beat her to death.

This is the tale I heard as a child and if you walk, on a moonless night, along the lane where she dwelt, between Ladywell Corner on the Southend Road and Grace's Cross. perhaps you may still see Moll Ram's ghost, though I doubt it for the thicket of furze has been replaced by a red brick dwelling and street lamps shine mercilessly where once a profusion of tansy graced the hedgerow.

In the second half of the last century the ghost of an old woman was said to haunt Pound Lane, Bowers Gifford. No story connected with the superstition has survived and I do not think that anyone ever saw it. The first village policeman thought he did, but discovered afterwards that it was a donkey in a ditch. He is reported to have said that "His helmet fairly wobbled on his head".

The entrance to Church Road, Basildon, from Clay Hill Road, was firmly believed to be haunted ninty years ago. This ghost was of a mischievous nature and was said to throw people over the hedge and into the fields. The occupier of Basildon Hall was one who said that he had had this unpleasant experience. So strong was the belief that men leaving the Bull Inn after dark would not go that way alone, but waited for company. There does not appear to be any story to account for the ghost, but it was a very lonely place with tall elms either side of the road and no houses in sight. Strangely enough I remember my father saying that, as a boy, he never liked that part of the road at night. Whether he had heard of the ghost I cannot say - if not, it seems as if there was something uncanny about that piece of road. A school now stands on one side and shops on the corner; some of the trees survive and mischievous spirits trouble no one. Another ghost said to haunt Church Road is that of a girl who was killed by being thrown from a trap or cart.

Three ill-attested ghosts haunt the roads of pretty Danbury village. A legendary Roman soldier is said to appear on the Common, perhaps the tale comes from the days when the Romans knew Danbury or it may be that the ghost was said to be that of a soldier and, in course of time, became known as a Roman soldier. The ghostly monks seen in Well Lane by two ladies were reported to have been walking along the road when they suddenly disappeared and have not been seen since. Some kind of spectre has also been seen at Moor's Bridge.

A curious experience at Danbury is told by Mr A Morrish of Chelmsford. Many years ago he was walking up Danbury Hill, wheeling his bicycle. He was almost at the top when he saw clearly another cyclist coming down the hill on the opposite side of the road. Behind the cyclist was a motor car and the headlamps gave a silhouette effect to the advancing rider. In a moment the car passed by and it was reasonable enough to expect the cyclist to do like wise seeing that the car driver was, when he first observed him, in the process of pulling out to overtake. But he never saw the cyclist pass nor on looking back was there a cyclist in sight. There were no side turnings on the right hand side at this particular spot neither was there, at that time, any overhanging foliage that might have given a false impression.

Not far away, at Little Baddow. In the early 17th century Sir Henry Mildmay brought his young and pretty wife, Alice, the daughter of Sir William Harris of Creeksea Place, to Grace's that had a magnificent avenue of trees called Grace's Walk. Lady Alice died in 1615; it is said that she drowned herself in a pond nearby because Sir Henry was unkind to her and that her ghost is to be seen by the pond on moonlight nights. Although 400 years have passed the tradition is still told in the surrounding villages, but there is no documentary evidence to support the tale of the unkind Sir Henry. According to another account the spirit of Lady Alice haunts Grace's Walk by the bridge crossing Sandon Brook. Her beautiful home still stands at the side of a charming little lane and her effigy may be seen in Little Baddow church. The fine avenue of trees, however, has been cut down and the wayside pond near the entrance to Grace's is silted up.

During the Second World War American troops were billeted here and the men were scared stiff to go on sentry duty. It is not recorded that they ever saw the ghost, but they were probably plied with tall stories by the local people, however, two riders could not make their horses pass a certain spot in Grace's Walk and had to make a detour. In the *Essex Review* of July, 1942, Cannon Jesse Berridge told how Mr Lee, a Chelmsford surveyor, wrote in his Common-Place Books of an apparition in Grace's Walk, in the first half of the 18th century: it does not, however, refer to Lady Alice. One summer day Mr Lee walked from Eve's Corner, Danbury, to Mr John Belcher's house at the lower end of Grace's Walk. Returning home about sunset he was walking on the horse way in the middle of the walk, it was not dark and he was, to the best of his knowledge and belief, in full possession of his senses. Soon after he had passed the bridge he saw his daughter, Mary, a child of about 7 years old, walking on the footpath between the trees and the hedge with her silk hat on and silk cloak such as she went about in. He was pleased that she had come to meet him and watched her cross the walk and thought that she was sitting down to wait for him he was then about twenty rods away. When he came up to the place she was not there upon the bench as he had expected nor could she have hidden herself. A man being on the opposite side of the hedge, Lee asked him if he had seen the little girl, but he said no. Mr Lee was dumbfounded, for if she had passed the man must have seen her. When he got home the girl was there and he did not mention anything about it as he believed it portended something good or evil. His daughter lived longer than he expected, dying at the age of 25 of smallpox at her brother's house in St George's in the Borough.

At Wakering there is the ghostly legend of Baker's Grave. A baker from Barling hanged himself from a tree that stood where three roads meet. He was, in the manner of those days, buried at the foot of the tree and his ghost somewhat disturbed the villagers for, on windy nights, his heels could be heard knocking together as if he still hung on the tree. When the moon shone whoever ran round the tree a hundred times was said to be rewarded by seeing the baker kneading his dough with his back to the tree. One person tried this with an unfortunate result; he tripped over a root of the tree and sprained his ankle before he completed his task: some thought it was a judgement for deriding the legend. The tree is long since gone and Council houses are built in the vicinity of this once lonely spot that local folks were frightened to pass.

Another story is that Baker's Grave or Baker's Corner, as it is now called, is haunted by Baker's big black dog. This is probably a fusion with another legend, that of the black dog of Star Lane, North Shoebury, not far away, and dating back to the time of the invasion by the Norsemen. Poor Rate was collected on Baker's Grave (probably the adjoining field) in 1723, so the legend is over two hundred and fifty years old at the very least. In *The Place Names of Essex* Baker's Grave is said to be probably associated with Clement de Bakere, 1314.

At Paglesham a ghost was said to haunt three hollow trees that stood in the bend of the road near East Hall. This was probably connected with the fact that the hollow trunks of the 'Three Old Widows', as they called them, were once used by smugglers and £200 worth of silk was once hidden in them. Only two trees now remain.

In a lane at Rayne in early spring the wayside dogwood bushes are stained with crimson; it maybe and probably is due to the soil, but local superstition says that it is memory of a murder that happened there one summer night and calls them 'bloodsticks'. The story is that in 1790 two Welsh drivers, John Jones and Robert Ellis, came to the well-known Bardfield Fair and sold their animals well. In the evening they left Bardfield, going in the direction of Braintree. They had plenty to drink, but at the next village they stopped at the inn for more beer and a quarrel broke out. The landlord intervening, they left the inn and continued on their way, leaving the high road. In a road leading to Rayne Jones struck Ellis a blow which stunned, but did not kill him. He then knifed him, hiding the body in a deep ditch covered with leaves and twigs. Jones returned to Wales where he told Mrs Ellis that her husband had died and been given a decent funeral. He then proposed marriage and the widow (over whom the quarrel had partly been) agreed to marry him after a suitable time had elapsed. However, it was not long before a constable appeared to ask Mrs Ellis to come to Rayne to identify some of her late husband's buttons and Jones had to answer a charge of murder. Some bullocks in an adjoining field had refused to go near a certain place in the hedge and the boy in charge of them noticed this and, on examining the place, found the body. Jones was found guilty and hanged.

It is not known that a ghost haunts Thieves' Corner, Roxwell, but there are two stories as to how it got its name. One is that a former owner of Boyton Hall was attacked by two thieves. He knocked their heads together and dumped them in a pond near the Corner. The other, and possibly the true story, is that it got its name because a sheep-stealer was hanged there. This tale was told 50 years ago, by a man of 80.

A Fobbing woman, Mrs Jean Clarke, had a very uncanny experience when she was driving her shooting brake to Bury St Edmunds one winter night in 1950; she believes she gave a lift to a ghost! [*Sunday Express*, 15

January, 1956] Her only companion was her cocker spaniel, sitting in the back of the car. She had pulled up to look at the map by the light of the dashboard when the dog began to howl. He stood up, his fur bristling and looked at the front passenger seat. Then she noticed a man sitting beside her, dressed in a very old-fashioned cloak collared fawn coat. It was too dark for her to see him clearly. He pointed forward and she assumed that he wanted a lift and was, perhaps, a simpleton, though it was strange that she had not seen or heard him enter the car, but she had been engrossed in the map. She drove on and, at the same time, the atmosphere in the car became very cold. After driving not more than 40 yards he made a sign for her to stop, which she did, when he vanished by just floating through the door. Mrs Clarke thought he must have opened the door quietly while her attention was occupied by driving. All the time her uninvited passenger was in the car the dog growled with his hair on end. She did not know until later that the incident had happened in Borley, where the famous haunted Rectory was situated. On hearing of the headless coachman said to haunt Borley she wondered if it was he she had given a lift to.

The busy High Street of Southend-on-Sea would not seem to be the place for unlikely experiences, but two strange stories can be told. The first is that of a lady who was walking by the Odeon Cinema when she saw a newsboy with a placard that stated there had been a bad rail crash with a number killed and injured. She was particularly shocked as her son was travelling on that line. She went to the station for further information, but was told there had been no crash. She said she had just seen the news on the placards, but was assured that no such thing had happened. They evidently thought she was either mad or drunk. She had never had such an experience before and, on her reaching home, her family remarked on her appearance. The next day there was a rail accident, as she had so unexpectedly foreseen, and the number of killed and injured were the same as she had seen on the placard.

During 1942, when Southend was evacuated and the High Street was always practically deserted, a lady and her daughter were shopping one Saturday afternoon. As they walked towards Victoria Circus, a young lady approached them with a badly swollen leg. The mother remarked to her daughter about the girl's leg, when suddenly an old lady wearing old-fashioned clothes appeared at their side and remarked, "Her leg looks bad, doesn't it?" The lady replied, "It certainly does." The old lady then pointed to Byatt's, the pork butchers, where there was a small queue and asked what they were waiting for. They turned to look at the queue, then glanced back at the old lady, but she had disappeared. There was not a person in sight.

The Southend Arterial Road has its ghost, said to be that of a girl killed in a car accident. She appears at Kent Elms Corner, muddy and bare-foot, and asks for a ride to Victoria Circus, Southend. Motorcyclists have given her a lift, only to find that she has disappeared before they reach their destination.

Then there is the very queer experience of a South Benfleet resident, who was walking in St Mary's Road, when she met two ladies coming down the road carrying a coffin between them. Strangely enough it did not seem to her at that moment to be a very unusual thing for them to be doing. She had passed them before it struck her as odd; she turned round immediately to find only one of the ladies walking along on her own - and no coffin! This strange tale had a sequel. About three weeks later the lady who had remained after her ghostly companion and their burden had disappeared died.

Many years ago a well-known and much-respected resident of South Benfleet, who had business premises in the village, was in the habit of travelling to Southend regularly to the wholesale merchants, always taking the shortest route up Vicarage Hill. His little van, drawn by a mare named Beauty, was a familiar sight. One day, when going up Vicarage Hill, as they approached a certain house the mare suddenly stopped and refused to budge; when cajoled, she wildly reared and signified her intention of going no further. Luckily her owner saw a man experienced in the ways of horses, who volunteered his services, but nothing would induce the mare to proceed and the only alternative was to turn round, drive down the hill and take the road up Bread and Cheese Hill instead. It was subsequently discovered that a man had committed suicide in that particular house. Did Beauty sense a tragedy or perhaps feel a supernatural presence?

A ghost walks the A13 at Vange. Mr John Howard, when he was licensee of the Five Bulls Inn, saw it. At an interview in the *Thurrock Gazette* of 26 September, 1969, he said, "There was always a lot of talk in the pub about a ghost. On several occasions from the upstairs bedroom I saw it.

"First I heard a thumping noise and then I saw the ghost. It was pure white and coming down the A13 from the direction of Vange Church and then it disappeared over in the direction of the Fobbing rail crossing. I know I saw it and nobody will ever convince me different."

Seventy years ago the pond at Rookery Corner, Stanford-le-Hope, was said to be haunted by a young lady who, wearing a three-cornered hat, rode a white pony through the pond at midnight.

A woman in a grey cloak is said to haunt Blacksmiths Lane, Orsett, on the old stage-coach road to London. The tradition is that a young couple many years ago were murdered by a highwayman and since then the girl appears from time to time near one of the milestones.

Creeksea Place

Apparitions of marshland and river

The Essex marshes, when the mist is rising on an autumn evening and at night, especially in winter with the cries of the wildfowl overhead, can be very eerie. Many ghostly tales told of the marshes are connected with smugglers and will-o'the-wisps.

In the second half of the last century farm hands were frightened to go on Pitsea Marshes at night because of strange lights, which they were convinced had ghostly origins, but were probably made by smugglers. Old Boosey, who lived on Vange Marshes, was frightened by a jack o' lantern, which was believed to be an omen of death. He did not know that the ghostly light was due to the spontaneous combustion of gases from decaying vegetable matter on marshy ground.

The village of Mucking, standing within half a mile of the Thames, had a tradition that has now died out. Ancient Mucking Hall was reputed to be haunted by the ghost of a suicide. During the last century the villagers would glance quickly at the windows when dusk fell, hoping, yet fearing, to see a face there. There was a strong belief that it had a secret tunnel once used by smugglers connecting it with the now-defunct Crown Inn and there was a shaft where contraband was concealed.

There still exists a belief among the older residents of the Southchurch area of Southend that the Glen in Southchurch Avenue was haunted. Built over a hundred years ago it was demolished in the 1960s. The man who built it in an old sandpit was thought to be a philanthropist. He had special cellars built; later he was found to be connected with smuggling and the legend is that it was the headquarters of a large gang. Not only did they smuggle, but they were also engaged in wholesale stealing from ships going up the estuary to London docks, with a speciality in ivory tusks. Members of the crew would throw them over board to some of the gang who came to the vessel in small boats. When eventually a police raid was made on the Glen a large amount of the stolen property was found in the deep cellars. No one has seen the ghost in recent years, but there still exists a belief in hidden treasure. Most likely the 'haunting' was really the smugglers' activities or they invented a ghost to keep folks away.

Many ruined farmhouses and cottages in Essex have the reputation of being haunted. Slatey House that stood in ruins isolated on Corringham Marshes in the 1930s was said to be definitely haunted, but, judging by its condition when visited by the author, cattle were the only spooks!

The marshland village of Paglesham had a haunted house that was recognised as such by the postal authorities. At one time it attracted hundreds of tourists and there were even picture postcards sold that showed a skeleton at one of the windows of the cottage, yet it is not known how it came to be haunted, if haunted it was, or why its fame spread. It was no doubt used by smugglers who found a ghost very useful. The cottage stood near Paglesham church and was thought to be 400 years old. Its beams were old ships' timbers. The last tenant did not appear to mind the ghost, for he lived there for 60 years.

Brandy Hole, on the Crouch at Fambridge, has the reputation of being haunted. One misty October, when it was almost dark, a yachtsman was going home when something went wrong with his car. With his head in the bonnet he was busy for some minutes and, when he straightened up, he found a man standing behind him. At first he thought it was his friend, then he noticed that the figure wore a blue sweater like a seaman, but there was no body to be seen below the waist! The friend who was sitting in the car did not see anything.

Benton, the local historian, tells a legend of the lonely isle of Foulness. Lucky Corner was said to be notorious with the inhabitants as the haunt of the parochial ghost, 'a woman without a head'. This tale is now dying out, but a policeman who had only been on the island a few months in 1951 told the author that at a certain spot he always had a curious feeling of being watched, although there was nothing on the road to account for it. Another policeman joined in the conversation and remarked that he had the same feeling at this spot at nighttime as me. Neither had mentioned this to one another before.

Foulness is and always has been a lonely island, a haunt of smugglers and other lawless persons, so the atmosphere of some dark deed may yet linger on. Before some part of the island was reclaimed a sailing ship was sunk just off the coast and the islanders swear that, in the right weather conditions, the ship can be seen today sailing through the field that was once tidal water. Then there is a certain pond haunted by a serving maid. The story goes that she became pregnant by her master: instead of supporting her, he threw her out, so she made for the nearest pond and drowned herself and she still walks round the pond - it is even said that she accompanies passers-by when they walk past it.

Canvey Island is, of course, quite different for it has a large population and is heavily built-up. An old Dutchman haunts Canvey. He was often seen wearing buckled shoes, full knee breeches with rosettes at the sides and had something slung over his shoulder. He always came from Benfleet in a northwest direction up Church Parade, through a garden on the way to Oysterfleet. The lady whose garden he passed through was washing some clothes one day when she saw the shadow of a very tall man, possibly eight feet tall, and wearing a pointed hat, through the frosted glass door, but when she opened the door no one was there. She also often heard his running footsteps at dusk along the old track by the sea-wall from Wintergarden to Waterside Farm; they stopped about the bend. Her husband also saw a figure walking through the verandah of the bungalow. The verandah was raised, the railing being about level with the window sill, and he saw the head and shoulders of a man. Had the man been walking on the verandah his head would have been above the sill and the apparition was, therefore, on ground level, as it would have been before the bungalow was built. One of the children saw the Dutchman in the garden and a servant would never have tea in the garden during the summer, but would not say why; it was thought she too had seen or heard something.

There is also a legend of a haunted house on the island. Two old gentlemen lived there; one was a believer in the Christian faith, the other an agnostic. The Christian said that, should he die first, he would come back and convince his unbelieving friend that there was a hereafter. He did die first and one night, when the wind was roaring wildly, there was a peculiar noise - the remaining old gentleman went to the door and opened it; the wind blew in, but nothing was to be seen, then the wind died away and the cat that had followed the man seemed to recognise someone and started to purr and rub against something it apparently both saw and felt, but still the old gentleman saw nothing! When part of the old house was demolished a secret chamber was found containing the remains of rusted horse pistols. One occupier of the house said that he heard strange noises, including footsteps, and at times the place became cold, although fires were burning.

At Knightswick Farm on Canvey a lady, hearing a strange noise, opened the door and saw a nun walking in the garden. She shut the door, but opened it again in time to see the nun disappearing into the ground. There is said to have been a chapel at Knightswick and there is also a legend that a tunnel led from the farm to Hadleigh Castle - most unlikely, as it would have to go under Benfleet Creek, otherwise it might be thought that the nun had disappeared at the former entrance to the tunnel.

A romantic tale used to be told about a young woman named Lucy, who worked at the 16th century Lobster Smack Inn on the Island. Lucy was engaged to Jack, a sailor. They were to be married at St Katherines, the village church, in the spring, but on a homeward voyage Jack was lost at sea. Lucy would not believe this, he would come back She said. As time went by Lucy, refusing all offers of marriage, pined away and when she died she was buried in her wedding dress in the village churchyard. In the spring Lucy was said to go down the Brides' Walk to the church and you know when she comes, said the old man who told the tale many years ago, because there is a powerful smell of violets. The Brides' Walk is now Hole

Haven Road and what was once a rough cart track with wild parsley growing on its banks, now has huge oil tankers dashing along the new road - there is little smell of violets now!

The village of Fobbing has several resident ghosts. The vineyards near the church is one haunted spot. Old residents have affirmed that a real old-fashioned ghost, complete with strange noises and clanking chains, can be heard here. It may be near here that the Priory mentioned in the story of Jack Straw's rising in the village was situated. The name is probably a survival from Norman days when there may have been vineyards on the south facing hill slope.

A friend who may be called 'a receiver' visited Fobbing one summer day. She and two friends sat on a gate near the wharf. She did not like the atmosphere, there was something she could not describe, but which she did not like about the spot and she said so to her friends. Then she felt someone or something push her in the back, throwing her to the ground. She assumed her friends had accidentally pushed her and accused them of so doing, but they emphatically denied touching her then she felt something touch her leg. The friends were mystified and they all left what my friend named as a sinister spot. Later it was learnt that suicide had been committed at some time in a nearby building. On another visit to Fobbing, the same lady stood near the church tower and, facing the hill leading down towards Corringham, she pointed out to her friend a gabled Elizabethan house. Her friend said she could not see such a house and a visit to the spot proved there was no house - yet my friend had distinctly seen it.

Black House, Leigh-on-Sea standing on the top of the

cliff facing east, where Broadway West now begins, was dreaded as being haunted. It was demolished in 1927, but two cedar trees planted in the grounds by John Loten can still be seen behind the shops on the top of Church Hill. Loten was Collector of Customs at Leigh for 33 years and lived at Black House from 1792 to 1815. Benton in *The History of Rochford Hundred* says, "Loten in deepening a cellar [at Black House] found under the stairs a human female skeleton which was reinterred in the churchyard." It was popularly believed that after this the ghost was laid, for it was no more heard of.

On all of John Wesley's visits to Leigh he stayed at the house of Dr Cook, a physician and member of a noted Leigh family; this house was said to be haunted by a troubled spirit and once was closed owing to public alarm. This was probably because the doctor believed in supernatural visitations and, when he died in 1777, he left references to the spirit world in his will, which may have set the superstitious inhabitants of the old town thinking and imagining things. This now-vanished 17th century house was very much altered in later years; its garden was taken by the railway and in its last days it was used as a restaurant. A room panelled in Spanish mahogany that had been closed for many years was opened in 1929.

Lapwater Hall, Leigh, that was said to be haunted by the ghost of a highwayman, had a good story connected with it. The house disappeared some years ago, but the name is perpetuated in Lapwater Close, near the site. The name Lapwater is said to have been given to it by the workmen who built it in 1751 and there are several versions of this story. The house stood on the site of an earlier residence called Leigh Park House and was in the

Georgian style, with a lower rambling wing of 1844. The original building was empty and tumbling down when a stranger named Gilbert Craddock bought it and ordered it to be hastily rebuilt. Gilbert caused considerable comment among the villagers as he was a very ugly, bad-tempered man with a squint and he owned a horse, Meg, without ears. The legend is that the workmen's wages included two pots of beer a day and when the owner came extra was expected, but Gilbert only cursed and would not grant it. When the last roof beam was fixed and they should have had extra beer Gilbert, who had arrived on his famous earless horse, refused their request and shouted, "Drunken dogs! Lapping all day - if you must lap, go to the pond and lap water." Whereupon the workmen christened the place Lapwater Hall.

Some time later excise men called at Lapwater Hall to search for the notorious Cutter Lynch, who proved to be none other than Gilbert Craddock. Gilbert indulged in smuggling as a side-line, but was really a highwayman. He was never caught, for witnesses could not identify the muffled figure on a large black horse and the Bow Street Runners could not prove that the horse was Craddock's mount, for witnesses said it had ears, while that ridden by Craddock had none. Gilbert used to fit false ears on the animal when he was on the road.

The end of Gilbert was that he was found drowned in the pond he had recommended to the workmen, but some say he was indicted by the excise authorities for swindling them and was hanged. He was condemned to haunt the Hall, inviting all to drink at his expense as punishment for being so mean to the workmen and, it is said that, a year after his death, when Nan Tricker who had helped the housekeeper of Lapwater Hall was married to Tim Ladds, the bride's father. Amos, went to the Hall to see how much beer was left and found, in the darkest part of the cellar, Gilbert squinting at him with a mug and spigot in hand, beckoning him to have a drink. Several good 'ale fellows' claimed to have seen his ghost, but no one has accepted his offer of a drink and it is said that he can have no rest until he can redeem in some way his fault of denying his workmen their share of ale.

The above is the most popular version of the story, but another is that, until it was demolished in the last century, Gilbert had to haunt the old pump, aimlessly cranking the handle and saying, "Let them lap water." Now Gilbert is probably at rest, his fault redeemed, as the ghost with the foaming tankard is no longer seen. The last occupiers, however, did say that footsteps were heard as one ascended the stairs, but that it might have been an echo caused by the way the house was built.

At Shoeburyness, there is an amazingly creepy tale of a haunted farm. Two boys are said to have spent a night in the loft of an empty house. During the night they woke up and heard angry voices. Looking through the trap door they saw everything lit up and a man and woman quarrelling, while they watched the man killed the woman, then all became quiet again and the light went out. The boys were too frightened to do anything that night, but in the morning, when they fearfully descended from the loft, the place was as empty and desolate as it had been on their arrival and there was no sign of any deed of violence. The marshes of Shoeburyness are reputed to be haunted by the ghost of an old man, who is in the habit of walking through them at certain unspecified times of the year.

The ancient causeway, the Strood, connecting Mersea Island with the mainland, built for the convenience of the Roman garrison at Colchester, is haunted by a Roman soldier. Mr H G Fulcher of East Mersea says he has often been seen. He can be observed upwards from the waist only as he walks on the original level of the road as the modern carriageway has been raised several feet. Years ago Mrs Jane Pullen, the landlady of the Peldon Rose, was crossing the Strood in moonlight when she heard the footsteps of the centurion ringing on the causeway behind her [J Wentworth Day: *Farming Adventure*].

Not far away is Mersea Mount on Barrow Hall Farm, which the Morant Club excavated in 1912, when a small tiled chamber was found. In it was a lead casket containing a pale green glass bowl, wherein were the ashes of a Roman who died in the first century - which may be those of the ghostly soldier. One story told of the Barrow is that three woman all desiring the same man either fought and killed each other or went out to sea together and were drowned. They were all buried together in a boat under the Barrow. This story may be genuine folklore or connected with the legend told in Sabine Baring-Gould's novel, *Mehalah*. This is still told on the island, but is not a genuine story. Two Danish brothers are said to have fought for the same girl, killing each other, and being buried with the boat in the Barrow. Every full moon they can be heard fighting in the ship's hold in the heart of the Barrow. The precincts of the Barrow are said to be haunted, but there is no particular story.

Ghosts of the Southend area

There are a number of reports of ghostly happenings in Southend-on-Sea and its surroundings, many of which are well-attested .

The spirit of a World War I veteran terrified a young mother and her children in a council house near Sutton Road in 1967. The family were almost forced to leave their home because of ghostly footsteps and banging, a disembodied voice and an old man visible only to a 4-year-old boy. Visitors heard heavy irregular footsteps across the floor upstairs, while the young wife and a neighbour saw coats come flying down the stairs and a rocking horse began to rock violently when no one was near. On one occasion the wife believed that someone had broken in and coats flew down the stairs and a light bulb was found on the floor, but there was no one upstairs, except the sleeping children, and no way for anyone to get out, but down the stairs.

The four-year old began talking about his friend 'who waited at the bottom of the stairs and walked him up'. This was put down to childish imagination until one night the mother felt someone standing behind her as she tucked the children into bed and heard someone call her name. She thought is was her imagination and took no notice, but that night the noises became louder and louder. At 9.30 the little boy screamed blue murder. "The man is lying by my bed cuddling me up," he said.

The wife's mother persuaded her to go to the

Spiritualists for help and they told her not to be afraid. The spirit was that of an old man, upset and frightened because he could not find his wife. He meant no harm. The house had stood empty for two years while the widowed tenant was in hospital. A seance was held in the house and the spirit said he could not leave his wife, but eventually agreed to go, but not before he said goodbye to the little boy. A description of the man given at the seance fitted that given by a neighbour who knew him when alive. He had only one leg and the husband remembered finding a medical certificate from the 1914-18 War among rubbish when they moved in. The spirit was felt to be in the house after the seance, but there were no more noises and the wife was no longer afraid.

A house in London Road, on the site of the present Eastern National Bus Station also harboured an apparition. A woman who worked there said that she and another employee used to see the figure of a woman on a landing going into a room that was never opened. It was thought she was a nurse. After a fire at Jackaman's Furniture Store the room was opened and was found to be a nursery with children's pictures stuck on the walls. Later it was found that the house had been a Salvation Army Home for Children.

A married couple living at Clifton Court, Royal Terrace, in 1966 were made very unhappy by ghostly happenings in their bedroom. A reporter from the *Southend Pictorial* who interviewed them said they looked as if they had seen a ghost and they assured him they had! On its first visitation one November night the wife awoke suddenly and saw a grey luminous shape near the end of the bed. It was a side view and she could see no face. She sat up and it vanished. There was no sound, but afterwards the room was as cold as ice. Nothing more happened until the following March when the husband heard the rustle of what appeared to be clothing in the hall, but found nothing. "It was a kind of swishing noise I heard," he explained. The very next morning at 5 o'clock in between bed and door was a cowled grey shape hanging in the air. "I could plainly see eye sockets," said the husband, "and the tip of a nose, nothing else. I called out 'What do you want?' and the thing disappeared at once. When it had gone and for a long time afterwards there was an unpleasant odour in the room, earthy and musty, which a spray did not remove." The next day the couple moved out of the bedroom and sought advice and, as a result, the vicar performed a service of exorcism in the bedroom. After that there was peace, but they were unable to forget it and would not use the room, so they decided to leave the flat.

In light and airy white-walled 18th century Prospect House, Leigh-on-Sea, the home of Mrs Vera Smith, JP, who was Mayor of Southend 1969/70, the ghostly figure of an 18th century man was seen by Mrs Smith on the stairs. Previously she had scoffed at such things, but the *Southend Pictorial* of August, 1962, reported that in the early hours of the morning she went to the bathroom and on the way back she glanced over the banisters 'quite idly and saw a figure on the stairs'.

"I saw him quite clearly. He was elderly and short and wore a long coat with knee breeches and stockings and his hair was tied back in a cue. I remember he was definitely bandy and wore heavy shoes and he was wobbling down the stairs. I didn't hear a sound. I realised afterwards that, although I could see clearly what he was wearing, it was all in black and white and the figure was blurred at the edges. I immediately realised from the costume that it was not a real person, but I had no sense of fear or cold chills. In a few seconds he had gone."

When Mrs Smith told her husband and daughter about the apparition they recalled a strange incident a few weeks earlier when a 4-year-old child of friends startled them by screaming with fear. Days later she told her mother what had frightened her, "There was a man standing in the corner". Mrs Smith has since told the writer that there is a distinctly fishy smell when the ghost is around.

The earliest records of the house show that in 1845 it was lived in by Thomas Bradley, surgeon and beer retailer. As far back as 1894 the ghost was common talk among the inhabitants. An old Leigh resident remembers how, shortly after that time, he went with his father to do some repairs at Prospect House and mend a well-cover in the basement and, while this was being done, his father warned him not to venture too far along the passages as the ghost lived at the end of one.

Southchurch Lawn, later Eton House School, has a history of nearly 900 years. There is said to have been a tunnel used in the 17th century for smuggling. Nelson and Lady Hamilton are supposed to have stayed here and, in 1801, 5-year-old Princess Charlotte, visiting Southend for health reasons, stayed at the Lawn and, while there, missed death by inches after running from the north door into the path of a horse, so it is not surprising that a ghost is said to haunt the north front of the house with a lantern.

In 1958 another of Southchurch's ancient houses was demolished to make way for a garage and car salesroom. The Oakes, Southchurch Road, once known as Tile House and shown on maps of about 1770, was reputed to be haunted by the ghost of a woman. Many years ago it was empty for a long period and there was much excitement in the village when the body of a woman was found in one of the rooms of the deserted building. She had been dead for a long time and was not known in Southchurch. Older residents claim that people have seen her ghost.

When a member of a local Sketch Club was cremated at the then-newly-built Crematorium in Sutton Road a club member who attended the service heard the quick tap, tap of high heels in a distinctive walk as she sat waiting with several other members for the ceremony to begin. She thought, "So Mrs - has made it," then remembered it was this lady's funeral she was attending. Another person also heard the heels tapping, although no one was seen.

Southchurch Lawn

Animal ghosts

Although stories of ghostly animals are not common in Essex there are several well-attested, as well as legendary beasts. The black dogs that haunt some Essex roads and lanes are connected with the Hound of Odin and go back to the time of the Norsemen who harried this part of the English coast. Some black dogs are said to be a death warning.

It is said that a ghostly black dog is sometimes seen crossing the road from Vange to Fobbing where there was an avenue of trees near White Hall Farm. The shadows of the trees no doubt helped the illusion.

The residents of Great Wakering also speak of the black dog of Star Lane, which their forefathers swore they had seen. The lane is named after a long-defunct inn; the beer of this hostelry possibly accounted for some of the black dogs!

A black dog runs on the coast road from Peldon to Tolleshunt D'Arcy and another travels the county boundary between Middleton in Essex and Boxford in Suffolk.

A white dog runs down Mistley Hill, near Manningtree; it foretells a death in the Norman family. It was seen in 1938 [*Transactions of the Folklore Society,* June, 1952].

Hatfield Peverel has a 'shaggy dog' story. Fifty years ago it was common knowledge that Shaen's Shaggy Dog walked between the two drive gates of Crix, owned from 1770 to 1858 by the family of Shaen. This was quite a friendly animal, but if annoyed its anger was terrible. A man driving a timber waggon with two horses struck at him with a whip and at once all were reduced to a smoking heap of ashes. Shaen's Dog has not been seen for many years. Miss T M Hope in *The Township of Hatfield Peverel* says it is rumoured that he died of spontaneous combustion at his first sight of a motor car.

Coming to the present, there is a well attested doggy ghost seen a. Kelvedon Hall, near Brentwood, the home of Rt Hon Paul Channon, MP. At Christmas, 1949, Bundi, an Austrian sheepdog that had been a pet of the family for 14 years, died. Members of the staff saw it a few weeks later. Nobody has stated in what form Bundi appears, but he turns up at all times. Sir Henry Channon did not see the ghost, but he was conscious of its presence. This ghost of a loved pet is not feared.

There is another phantom dog that haunts the derelict 18th century church hard by Kelvedon Hall. Over 90 years ago the tenant of Germains was named French and the squire was Carington Wright. French did a little poaching and one evening, when he was out with his dog, the squire gave chase. The dog ran into the church and the squire followed it and shot it in front of the altar. Squire Wright was fined for desecration and the church had to be reconsecrated. The ghost of the dog, so legend says, has often been seen running round the church and entering the porch.

Mention should be made here, although it does not come under the heading of this Chapter, of the bad luck of Kelvedon Hall. The Hall, a red brick mansion built in George II's reign, was said to be an unlucky house when Sir Henry Channon came to live In it in 1937. Its bad luck, however, only began when the nuns of St Benedict occupied it. From 1932 to 1937 it was known as St Michael's Catholic School, but the nuns left after a series of tragedies.

First, a child fell in the playground and died within a week with tetanus. Later a workman was injured and, as the Community was not insured, they had to pay him 12s. 6d a week for life. A few weeks afterwards a little girl, who had been with the convent for nine years, was seized with pneumonia and died. In February, 1936, Sister Primavesi was found drowned in the lake, her hands clasping a crucifix. Nine months later, a guest, Mrs Gallivan, was found dying on the lawn after falling 30 feet from a bed room window. Sisters were sawing wood, when a chip flew off and struck one in the eye. For three days her life was in the balance and, although she recovered, her sight was permanently affected. The nuns were glad to leave this house that seemed to have a curse on it and, when they left, the Mother Superior, Sister D'Alton, is reported to have commented, "We are unanimous in the feeling that there is something terrible about the place. Since the day we came we have never felt happy. The convent seems to have some evil influence over us. It is uncanny to the last degree."

From 1538 the Hall was owned by the Catholic family of Wright. Ten John Wrights in succession lived in the house, then a baby was christened John Francis Wright; he died unmarried and was succeeded by his nephew, Edward Carington. After the direct succession of John Wrights was broken it seemed that the family's luck ran out. Edward was the last of the Wrights to live at Kelvedon.

One newspaper called it 'The House that Hates Women' and pointed out that there had always been a master of the house and it was only when women took it over that the bad luck began. When the Channons bought the Hall they took the precaution of having it blessed by the Bishop of Brentwood and its atmosphere of bad luck has long disappeared. There is a pond in the grounds where the ghost of a suicide who died some 50 years ago is said to appear, but it has not been seen recently.

At the marshland village of Great Wakering a white rabbit is said to haunt the corner by the church. Whether there is any connection between this and the four (formerly five) inns in the village one cannot say. One old fellow used to be so helpless after visiting the local that his horse used to take him home on its own. This man declared that, on one occasion, he was chased near the churchyard by a big black bear with red eyes - and no wonder!

Mrs M Bettany often spoke to a beautiful ginger kitten at her grocers in South Benfleet. On a Tuesday in January, 1956, she went into the shop, which was empty at the time; the door to the stock room was open and the dog stood by it. She saw the cat come from within the room, pass the dog and come towards the end of the counter. She moved to the counter to speak to it, but no cat was there. She thought it had perhaps gone beneath the counter and was looking over to see if it had when the shopkeeper arrived. "I'm looking for your kitten, he has just gone under the counter, I believe," she explained. "You could not have seen it, it was killed last Friday," she was told - but she had seen it!

Lastly, one Essex inn has a doggy ghost. The Thatchers Arms at Great Warley has a reputed ghost of a black Labrador dog.

The bar of Rayleigh Lodge (page 64)

Index

Aldridge, John 76
Ashard, G 13
Ashingdon 19,66
Audley, Sir Thomas 31
Aveley 85
Barclay, Rev D B 19
Barker, Nobby 46
Barking 46
Barling 112
Basildon 11,26,80,109
Bateman, Canon 66
Battlesbridge 80
Bayly, Miss E S 45
Bazille-Corbin, Rev Dr J E 2,17
Beche, Johannes 49
Beeleigh 96
Belcher, John 112
Bendlowes, William & Eleanor 76
Benfleet 72
Benfleet Art Club 79
Benton, Philip 23,121,125
Berechurch 31
Berridge, Canon Jesse 112
Bettany, Mrs M 16,137
Biddulph, Sir Theophilus 74
Billericay 8,42,54,81,108
Binney, Sir George 102
Blake, Mrs M 109
Bobbingworth 88
Boleyn, Anne 101
Bonner, Edmund 14
Boreham 101
Borley 13,65,115
Bowers Gifford 15,109
Bradfield 107
Bradley, Thomas 132
Bradwell-Juxta-Mare 65

Braintree 15,19,114
Brentwood 60
Brightlingsea 23,28
Broomfield 71
Brown, Samuel 23
Bull, Ethel 14
Bures 107
Bury, Betty 36
Bury, Bradford 37
Cambridge, Duke of 102
Canewdon 25,89
Canute 19
Canvey 122
Cartwright, W C 91
Castle Hedingham 41
Challis, Mrs 39
Channon, Paul 135
Charlotte, Princess 132
Chelmsford 60,73
Chigwell 91
Chilvers, Mrs 31
Chrishall 104
Clark, Mrs F B 11
Clarke, Mrs Jean 114
Claro, Fred 86
Clavering 23,90,104
Clothier, Mr 69
Coggeshall 100
Colchester 35
Cook, Dr 125
Cook, John 79
Coope, Octavius Edward 31
Copford 14
Corringham 120,124
Craddock, Gilbert 126
Cranwell, Mrs 104
Creeksea 111
Cressing 15
Cromwell, Oliver 67,84
Crook, B L Lester 5

D'Alton, Sister 136
Dagenham 106
Danbury 8,70,110
Dapifer, Eudo
Daren, James 27
Dengie 1
Dimsdale, Sir Joseph 83
Disbrow, Benjamin 67
Dixon, Thomas & Robert 71
Downham 67
Earls Colne 64,99
East Mersea 62
Edmond Ironside 19
Edwards, J 34
Elizabeth I 75,86
Ellis, Robert 113
Elphinstone, Canon M 66
Everard, Lady 73
Fambridge 120
Faulkbourne 75
Finchingfield 41
Fitzgeorge, George 57
Fobbing 114,117,124,134
Foulness 121
French, Mr 135
Fulcher, H G 37,128
Fyfield 39
Gallivan, Mrs 136
Gant, Mr 34
Georg, Prince 20
Gloucester, Duke of 97
Godfrey-Bartram, P B 25
Grays 81,93
Great Baddow 60,108
Great Bardfield 75,108,114
Great Burstead 7,57
Great Easton 103
Great Oakley 63
Great Wakering 11,37,77,112,134,137
Great Waltham 61,73

Great Warley 137
Great Wigborough 45
Great Yeldham 93
Grene family 86
Grey, Lady Katherine 75
Grimston, Sir Harbottle 107
Hadleigh 50,79,89,99
Hamilton, Emma 63,132
Harlackenden, Richard 99
Harris, Sir William 111
Harwich 63,91
Hatfield Peverel 134
Havering 22
Hawkwell 46
Hemming, Rev 13
Hemmings, Mrs Martha 50
High Laver 102
Hockley 25,78
Hodgeskynne, John 27
Hope, Miss T M 135
Hornchurch 22,82
Howard, John 117
Hughes, Richard 93
Hunter, William 61
Hutton 75,81
Ingatestone 58,74
James I & VI 96
Johnson, John 65
Jones, John 113
Jones, Johnny 82
Jones, Kenneth O 82
Jones, Rowland 82
Jordan, Richard 87
Joslin, John 24
Kelly, Rev N J 89
Kelvedon 84,135
Kelvedon Hatch
Kemble, Thomas 12
Kempe, William 41
Kipling, Rev C S 13

Kirk, Mrs 68
Kirstermann, Captain 88
Knights, Edward S 36
Ladds, Tim 127
Lamarsh 107
Langdon Hills 83
Latchford family 92
Latchingdon 36
Latton 96
Laurence, Ida 92
Lay, Susan 80
Lee, Atte 10
Lee, Sir Charles 73
Lee, Mary 112
Leigh-on-Sea 124,131
Lennard, Sir Thomas Barrett 85
Leroy, Charles 56
Leytonstone 59
Liberty, H P 6
Linford 46
Little Baddow 41,111
Little Burstead 38
Little Hallingbury 62
Little Oakley 69
Little Sampford 86
Little Wakering 36
Lloyd, Rev B 27
Loten, John 125
Loughton 108
Lynch, Cutter 126
Lynch, Simon 17
Maldon 8,28,59
Maley, Rev E A B 21
Manningtree 134
Manuden 64
Masham, Abigail 102
Mashbury 61
Matthews, Bryan 64
Mersea Island 62,128
Meyer, P H 88

Middleton 18,134
Mildmay, Sir Henry & Lady Alice 111
Mistley 134
Morley, F V 62
Morrish, A 15,80,110
Mount Bures 107
Mucking 119
Murgatroyd, M H 79
Murray, B 38
Nelson, Horatio 63,91,132
Nevinson, Nick 63
Newman, J H 107
Norman Family
North Benfleet 81
North Shoebury 113
Oliver, Rev 88
Orsett 118
Osyth, Saint 94
Owen, Mrs 65
Paglesham 113,120
Parson, D D 63
Patteshall Family
Payne, Terry 91
Peacock, Christopher 17
Peldon 128,134
Perkins, Sir William 73
Petre family 74
Phillips, Mrs E L 39
Pitsea 92,119
Pleshey 97
Pope, Fred 67
Price, Harry 14
Primavesi, Sister 136
Prittlewell 23,46,97
Pryse, Mrs 91
Pullen, Mrs Jane 128
Pyne, Henry 74
Rainaldus 2
Ram, Maria 108
Rayleigh 64,92

Rayne 23,60,108,113
Richman, Mr 43
Rochford 37,101
Romford 22
Roxwell 114
Runwell 2,12,17,48
Saffron Walden 104
St Osyth 94
Sanderson, Mrs 1 89
Sandon 109
Schilling, Sgt 70
Selletto, John 23
Sewardstone 102
Shaen family 134
Shaw, Misses 66
Sheldrake, 'Old' 36
Sheppard, Rev W J L 19
Shoeburyness 39,127
Smith, Peter 91
Smith, Mrs Vera 131
Smythe family 31
South Benfleet 63,67,116,137
South Weald 58
Southchurch 66,119,132
Southend 16,25,29,68,78,115,129
Sparvel-Bayly, J A 54
Spencer, Garry 25
Springfield 74
Stanford-le-Hope 93,118
Stansgate Priory 1
Stansted Mountfitchet 70
Steeple 1,11
Steeple Bumpstead 79
Stigand, Archbishop 20
Stondon Massey 87
Sulyard, Sir Edward & Lady Anne 17
Sutton, Thomas 62
Sutton 66
Tabor, Mrs V 66
Taylor, Mrs 33

Thaxted 102
Theydon Mount 40
Thoby 98
Thorrington 11,28
Thundersley 12,21,39,81,89,92
Thurston, George 70
Tilbury 63
Tilty 94
Tolleshunt D'Arcy 134
Tolleshunt Knights 9
Tonge, Susannah 48
Tricker, Amos 127
Tricker, Nan 126
Turpin, Dick 68,108
Vange 11,91,117,119,134
Vaughan, Miss E 107
Virley 9
Wallasea Island 11
Waltham 93,95
Walton on the Naze 22
Warwick, Countess of 103
Well, Barry 79
Wesley, John 125
West Ham 102
West Mersea 71
West Thurrock 64
Wethersfleld 74
Wheel family 92
White, Mrs Charlotte 34
White, George 48
White Roding 62
Wickford 2,6
Wickham Bishops 109
Witney, Harry 21
Wix 10
Woodley, Richard & Oliver 78
Wormingford 107
Wright, Edward Carington 135
Wright, John 136